Broken to Brave

Broken to Brave

Your Courageous Act of Healing
After Intimate Betrayal

Tammy Gustafson, MA, LPC

Revell

a division of Baker Publishing Group
Grand Rapids, Michigan

© 2026 by Tammy Gustafson

Published by Revell
a division of Baker Publishing Group
Grand Rapids, Michigan
RevellBooks.com

Printed in the United States of America

Library of Congress Cataloging-in-Publication Control Number: 2025021543
ISBN 9780800746551 (paper)
ISBN 9780800747909 (casebound)
ISBN 9781493452736 (ebook)

The names and details of the people and situations described in this book have been changed or presented in composite form in order to ensure the privacy of those with whom the author has worked.

This book is for informational and educational purposes only and does not constitute professional counseling, therapy, or coaching. The author, though a licensed counselor and coach, provides general insights that may not apply to individual situations. No therapeutic relationship is established by reading this book. Readers should seek qualified professional help for personal or marital issues. The author and publisher disclaim liability for any adverse effects arising from the use or application of the information contained in this book.

Cover design by Chris Kuhatschek
Stained glass image generated with Midjourney

The author is represented by the literary agency of Pape Commons.

Baker Publishing Group publications use paper produced from sustainable forestry practices and postconsumer waste whenever possible.

26 27 28 29 30 31 32   7 6 5 4 3 2 1

Contents

Foreword

When I was walking through my own story of betrayal, there were very few therapists who understood how to treat partner betrayal trauma. There were only a couple of books about the topic, and finding good help was like searching for that proverbial needle in the haystack.

Much has changed since then. Today there are books, workshops, conferences, podcasts, programs, and so many other wonderful resources for betrayed partners. The field has literally boomed in recognition of and response to the need.

However, when you are a betrayed partner and discovery first happens, you don't know about the world of resources and the community of help that's available. You're at the very beginning, reeling from the shock of learning that the one you love has so deeply hurt you and destroyed your safety and trust. You feel alone, like no one else could possibly understand the spin cycle of horror you've been thrown into.

For every betrayed partner, there is a road to travel between the point of discovery and the point of accessing help and support. There is a gap between "I'm alone in this nightmare" and "Someone has my hand."

My hope for every betrayed partner is that they would find this book to help them bridge that gap. This book is the primer you need to help guide you through all the stages of betrayal, because healing from betrayal trauma is a multiphase process, with each phase requiring different information and support.

Tammy intertwines her personal journey of healing and her professional work with betrayed partners as she reaches out to take your hand and shepherd you through the process of recovering and rebuilding after betrayal. While she provides expert guidance and direction, the biggest gift she offers is an enormous, loving dose of permission.

That includes permission to be exactly where you are in your experience. Permission to feel all the feels. Permission to be confused, to be uncertain, to not know the answers to the big questions, to be angry, to be hopeful, to need space and time, to need comfort, to be afraid. Tammy gives you permission to make the decisions that are best for you, providing you with key things to consider as you sit with your wisest self and weigh your options.

As she guides you through the healing process, she also provides space for you to inhabit your personal journey. While betrayed partners share many commonalities, each person is also navigating their own unique story and circumstance. Tammy's nuanced understanding of the issues gives you permission to see the lighted path ahead while negotiating your way forward along it.

Tammy is a beautiful, knowledgeable pathfinder, and this book is her way of reaching out to take your hand in hers. You are not alone. Someone has you. Lean into the support and guidance ahead.

Michelle Mays, LPC, CSAT-S

Preface

No one prepares you for betrayal.

Then, when it happens, it shatters life and everything you thought to be true. Suddenly, it's like you don't know which way is up, if you are moving forward or backward, or if it is even possible to heal.

I've been there. I get it.

I want you to know that there is a way through. I am not going to lie. The path of healing after intimate betrayal is the most painful, grueling path you may ever take, but it is worth fighting for yourself. Whether or not your relationship makes it, you are worth it.

On the other side there is beauty, joy, and adventure again. It is possible to be a stronger, even fuller version of yourself than you've ever been. It's okay if you don't believe me, but it's true.

First, though, we need to start exactly where you are at. One step at a time. One foot in front of the other.

I cannot take your pain away or calm the storm you are in, but this book is meant to be a companion and a guide along the way. I will offer you direction, encouragement, and empowerment. I will point you in the right direction when the waves feel too big and block your view of the shore. I will point out rocks to avoid that could take you out and currents that could pull you under. No matter how long you've been swimming or how far from shore you feel, there is a way through.

I wear three hats in this book: counselor, drawing from over fifteen years of clinical experience; coach; and fellow traveler, having swum the waters of betrayal myself. I will weave in and out of these three roles throughout these pages.

To be honest, I was never one of those women who wanted to use her story for good. When life blew up, I often said that my story could die a thousand deaths. I didn't want to tell anyone outside a small circle of trusted friends. Over time and after much healing, though, helping betrayed partners has become a passion.

In putting this book out to the world, I offer it as a lifeline for those who come behind me. There is no one right way to heal. I do not pretend to have all the answers or to have everything figured out, but I offer what I know. Take what is helpful, leave the rest, and know that I am cheering you on.

My hope for you is that you will feel seen, heard, understood, and empowered on your journey. There is a good life ahead. There is joy, beauty, and adventure waiting for you. It is possible, and I'm reaching out to help you through.

Warmly,
Tammy Gustafson

Introduction

Half-eaten chicken nuggets were scattered across the floor of my minivan, and the faint whiff of a diaper lost under a seat somewhere permeated the air. I didn't notice any of it that day. I stared absently past the dust on the dashboard.

I looked down at my journal. It read: *There's a very real chance that my marriage will end in divorce.*

You see, two months prior and almost ten years into what I thought was the perfect marriage, I found out that my husband had betrayed me. It shattered me.

Everything I thought I knew about him and our relationship suddenly felt like a lie. I didn't even recognize myself. I was confused, sad, and so angry. It felt like I was free-falling through a black hole, and I didn't even know if it was possible to get to the other side. Or if this—in all my pain and anger—was who I had become.

As I sat in my minivan that morning, though, I noticed a flicker of something inside me. It was a fragile resolution that I was going to make it—whether my marriage made it or not. I was going to heal. I was going to be okay.

In the following months and years, I leaned into healing and processing the pain. I joined a support group. My husband and

I went to counseling. I honored my anger and put it into words. I set boundaries and took the space I needed. I did not rush into forgiveness, but I eventually opened my heart to forgive and to free myself. It was a long, messy journey, but I made it. We made it as well.

That was over ten years ago. There is still dust on my dashboard and half-eaten chicken nuggets scattered across the floor of my minivan, but life looks very different today.

I did heal. I am no longer angry or sad. Life is good. I discovered new parts of myself along the way. I now know at the core of my being that I am strong, and I experience beauty, joy, and adventure again.

When I look at my life now, I don't see the broken pieces anymore; I see a beautiful mosaic—a unique, colorful, bold, playful, and powerful new creation that I designed. I will never be thankful for betrayal, but I am proud of who I have become.

You can heal too. You can pick up your shattered pieces and create your own unique, beautiful mosaic—whether your relationship makes it or not. It is possible. There is a good life ahead for you.

The Betrayal Healing Phases

There are four phases of healing after betrayal. I call them the Betrayal Healing Phases. I developed them based on my clinical and personal experience to help betrayed women through this process. The phases follow the relationship path after life shatters and provide practical help and guidance along the way. Think of them as guideposts, helping you to know that you are headed in the right direction.

When my life shattered, I had no idea what to do. I didn't know how to pick up the sharp fragments or if it was even possible to create something new. There is a way through, though, and this is the road map I wish someone would have shown and described to me:

Phase One: Reveal—Uncovering the truth about what your partner has done.

Phase Two: Rumble—Processing the heartbreak, stepping into your power, and waiting to see if your partner will do the work to heal.

Phase Three: Realign—Adjusting to the reality of the direction your relationship is headed.

Phase Four: Rebuild—Focusing on your healing and your relationship with yourself.

Throughout the phases, I'll help you navigate common questions betrayed partners wrestle with, including

When is it safe to trust again?
Do I stay or go?
How do I know I have the full truth?
What do I do with all of this pain?
Am I being gaslit?
How do I know if he is doing the work needed to heal?
Will our relationship survive? Do I even want it to?

It is important to understand what phase you are in and to learn what to focus on in each phase. Doing so will help you move through healing as smoothly as possible. I will also point out things not to focus on in certain phases, so you don't get stuck.

Of course, healing is never as neat and fast as we'd like it to be. It is possible to be in more than one phase at a time. Unfortunately, it is also possible to cycle back through the phases if your partner relapses. You are welcome to read about all the phases, but keep in mind that each phase is written specifically for those in that phase. So take what is helpful and leave the rest or come back to it later. This is a resource and guide for your entire journey.

> *Focusing on the wrong thing at the wrong time can shut down your healing process.*

This book is for all betrayed partners, no matter your relationship status, age, religious background, or demographic. I use the pronouns "she" and "her" and focus on women as the betrayed partner, but I recognize that many men are betrayed by their partners as well, and you are welcome here. At times, I will address issues specific to those who come from a faith background. If that doesn't fit for you, then skip it and move on. Everyone is welcome and respected here.

It doesn't matter whether you found out about your partner's betrayal yesterday or you are decades in, whether you are somewhere in the messy middle and not sure how it's going to end, whether you are divorced, or whether there's been a tremendous amount of healing in your relationship but you still feel like you've lost parts of yourself in the process. No matter where you are, you will find yourself in the four phases.

The focus of this book is *unapologetically* on *you* and *your* healing journey. Not your partner's or your relationship. I'll walk you down the path that the relationship follows, but ultimately this book is focused on *your* healing. I want to encourage you that no matter where you are now, as you lean into healing, you can become a stronger, deeper, fuller version of yourself—a woman who lives with the unshakable knowledge of her worth.

Survey

My desire for this book, and the overall work that I do, is to empower and give voice to betrayed partners. As a result, in partnership with Dr. Barbara Steffens, Dr. Janice Caudill, and Nii Codjoe,

I created a 35-question survey titled Healing After Betrayal (HAB). There were 1,729 betrayed partners from 25 countries around the world who completed the survey. The vast majority identified as white, heterosexual women between the ages of 20 and 80. Approximately 64 percent were still married to the person who betrayed them, 20 percent were separated, and 7 percent were divorced.[1] Their words and the results of the survey are sprinkled throughout the book. I'll refer to it as the HAB survey.

Special thanks to everyone who took the survey. Your input is important, and I am so grateful to you.

Core Foundations

As we start this journey together, I want you to know this is a shame-free zone. I have deep compassion for those who have experienced betrayal. My desire is to come alongside you to help strengthen, encourage, and empower you. To start, I offer three foundations for you to hold on to that will set the stage for everything to come.

Foundation 1: It Is Not Your Fault

Let's settle this right away. When you first find out about your partner's intimate betrayal, it is common to think there is something you did or didn't do to cause it. I want you to know that it is not your fault. You may struggle with the thought that if you were prettier, skinnier, younger, or had bigger boobs, this might not have happened. Almost every woman who has experienced betrayal struggles with this. It's normal. But *it is not your fault.*

Your partner alone bears the responsibility for his choices. No matter what was going on in your relationship, when he decided to step outside the relationship, it was his choice. Was the relationship

1. The remainder reported they were dating (2%), engaged (1%), widowed (<1%), broken up (1%), or other (4%).

perfect? No. They never are. Were there issues in the relationship? Perhaps. But even if there was something he was unhappy with, there are a thousand different things he could have done to address the issue. Instead, he chose to step outside the relationship, and that is 100 percent on him.

Foundation 2: You Have Great Worth and Value

It does not matter what your partner has or has not done. It doesn't matter whether you are in a relationship, married, divorced, single, or widowed. It doesn't matter what others think about you or your relationship. It doesn't even matter what your past has been, the mistakes you've made, or the lies you've been told about yourself. You don't need to fight for your worth or try to prove it. *You have great worth and value simply because of who you are. Period.*

Foundation 3: You Can Heal

Sometimes, when the pain and anger are so big, it feels impossible that you will heal and be at peace again. It is possible. It is not determined by whether your partner does the work to heal—though it is easier if he does. I truly hope your partner does the work to get clean and healthy. I hope he digs in and becomes a man of integrity who honors your heart and helps you heal. I hope your relationship becomes all you've wanted it to be and you get the redemption story—if that's what you want. But you can be okay and learn to thrive no matter what he chooses to do or not do. You can make it through whether your relationship survives or you are already divorced. *You can heal.*

Fear of Doing It Wrong

Many women are afraid of doing something wrong and messing up the healing process. I understand that feeling of desperately wanting to heal. Here's the secret though: There is no "right" way to heal. There is not one specific path. No one's method—including mine—is the only way to heal.

For example, a full therapeutic disclosure[2] is a valuable tool for helping him step out of the shadows and live in full transparency so that you can be given what you have always deserved and what your relationship has always needed—the truth. But do you have to use that specific tool or intervention in order to heal? No. Our disclosure process was a mess. It was a drip disclosure drawn out over what felt like months, with me grilling him and dissociating on a regular basis. But you know what? In the end I got the truth. I don't necessarily recommend doing it that way, but we still healed and I found my strength and power in the midst of it.

I say this to give you freedom. Again, there is no one right way to heal. Other professionals and I will offer you suggestions and guidance, but they are just that—suggestions and guidance. You get to decide what is best for you and your relationship. Own your journey. Step into your power. Ask for what you want and need. Trust your gut.

I'm honored to join you on your healing journey. I will show you how to pick up the sharp pieces of broken glass, make sense of the mess, and start to design your own beautiful mosaic that will be a reflection of the beautiful, valuable, empowered woman you are. Here we go. Let's do this together.

A Letter of Encouragement

Several years ago, I wrote a letter to myself as part of my own healing journey. It contained the words I wish I would have heard on the day life blew up. I now offer it to you. Feel free to write your name in the space provided and soak it in.

2. More about full therapeutic disclosures in Phase One.

Dear _____,

Hold on. This is going to hurt. It will hurt deeper, longer, and harder than you have ever hurt before.

And you will survive.

You are going to make it to the other side. It is possible. You will be stronger and deeper than you ever could have imagined.

You will be okay.

And don't worry about this story of yours. Just keep breathing and it will write itself.

So step in.

I know that you are scared. And I know that you are courageous. I am on the other side, and life is good. You don't have to fear pain. I'm sorry that you will have to feel it, but you don't have to fear it.

And remember . . .

You are beautiful.

You are loving.

You are strong.

You are loved.

You are enough.

Now go.

Tammy

Phase One

Reveal

The Shattering

Betrayal shatters you. Your heart—and everything you believed to be true—breaks into a million pieces. These fragments are all that remain of the life you once knew. Each shard is sharp and painful. Your heart is broken. Your relationship is broken. Everything feels shattered.

In Phase One: Reveal, the reality of the intimate betrayal is revealed, and you take your first steps along the road of healing. The goal of this phase is to get the truth about what your partner has done, which gives you the truth about your life and relationship.

In the next three chapters, I'll walk you through Phase One. I'll help you unpack what happened and the extent of the damage, and I'll give you tools to navigate common situations in this phase. I'll also help you know what to focus on and potential areas where you could get stuck.

1

Grounding in the Crisis

Betrayal is a "life before" and "life after" event. It is painful and life-altering. Let's start by getting clear about what intimate betrayal is. At its core, it is a break in the relationship agreement, whether spoken or unspoken. The breach in the relationship may or may not involve a sexual act with another person. It could be a hookup, emotional affair, prostitutes, dating apps, porn, strip clubs, or checking out other women, to name a few examples. The exact line of a relationship agreement may look different for each couple, but when a line is crossed, it is felt deeply.

The reality is that while intimate betrayal can come in many different forms, it always includes some degree of hiding—secrets and lying—either by what was said or what wasn't said. And it always involves an imbalance of power. Knowledge is power, so if your partner withheld information about what he was doing, he had the power. Or perhaps you knew about what was going on but he refused to stop—he had the power there as well.

> *Intimate betrayal always includes*
> *an imbalance of power.*

Many betrayed partners are given the message that they are overreacting and what happened was not that big of a deal. This puts you in the painful, confusing position of having to fight for your reality. This is particularly common around the issue of pornography. Society says that porn is not a big deal and that "boys will be boys," but if that was not agreed upon or acceptable in your relationship, then it is betrayal. So, to be clear, if you feel that your relationship agreement—spoken or unspoken—has been broken, then you have experienced intimate betrayal.

It is also important to note that abuse occurs in a significant percentage of relationships in which there is intimate betrayal. It is a deeply complicating factor that needs specialized support and attention. If your partner is physically abusive or if you are scared for yourself or your children, then I encourage you to pause and get specialized help for the abuse before implementing what's in this book. Confronting an abusive man usually increases the abuse. *Your safety—and the safety of your kids—is most important and comes before anything else.*

What Is Healing?

What does it mean to heal after betrayal? Does it mean your relationship or marriage comes out intact at any cost? Does it mean you immediately divorce him? Does it mean you're never triggered or that you never think about the betrayal again?

I want to offer my definition of what it means to heal so that you know where I'm taking you and can decide if you want to join me on this path. Two of the words I hear most often from betrayed partners to describe how they feel inside are "shattered" and "broken." I certainly felt that way when life blew up for me. Imagine the image of a mirror that was once whole and beautiful but now is scattered across the floor in a thousand pieces. Not only is it not whole, there is separation between the parts that were once whole and connected. Betrayal results in violent separation and disconnection within the relationship and internally for the person who was betrayed. Peace is gone. Confusion reigns. Pain is overwhelming.

Healing for a person who has been betrayed is finding a sense of wholeness again. It does not deny the reality or impact of what happened. Instead, it is valuing yourself enough to lovingly and compassionately pick up the pieces of your broken heart, tend to your wounds, discover your strength, and choose to create a beautiful and intricate—though perhaps complicated—mosaic work of art. It is facing the pain of healing in order to cultivate peace and wholeness (Dan Siegel calls it integration[1]) within yourself.

Healing is finding a sense of wholeness again.

This is the healing that can happen within you. It is also possible for the relationship to heal—if you want that and if your partner does the deep work of healing. However, you can heal even if he— or the relationship—doesn't. As I mentioned earlier, this book and the phases we'll discuss follow the path of the relationship, so we will certainly talk about your partner and your relationship. But the focus of this book is unapologetically on *you*. This book is about *you*.

1. Daniel Siegel, *The Neurobiology of "We": How Relationships, the Mind, and the Brain Interact to Shape Who We Are* (Sounds True, 2011), audiobook.

The Day Life Changed

The day you find out about the intimate betrayal is commonly referred to as Discovery Day or D-Day. You may have been blindsided and not known that anything was going on, or you may have seen signs but dismissed them. D-Day may not have been the first time the truth peeked its head out, *but it is the first time that something changed inside of you*. It's the day that his actions could no longer be ignored.

Regardless of the details, the backstory, or what brought you to that place, this is a significant turning point in your journey and the trajectory of the relationship. This is true no matter what the details of the situation are or how you learned about his acting out. Few things are more soul-crushing than finding out your partner has been unfaithful. It shakes the very foundation of your reality. It is overwhelming and disorienting. Nothing feels sacred, and everything feels undone.

Initial Impact

Betrayal hits the very core of who you are. It fundamentally changes not just your relationship but the way you experience yourself and the world around you—physically, emotionally, and mentally. No matter when your D-Day happened—whether it was yesterday or ten years ago—it's important to understand and process the initial impact.

Physically, your body experiences betrayal as *severe danger*, so the amygdala (your brain's ever-watchful danger sensor) immediately triggers your body into *fight, flight,* or *freeze* mode. Stress hormones flood your body. Your heart starts racing. Oxygen is routed to the most vital organs. At the same time, you might feel like someone is sitting on your chest and you can't get a full breath. Nonessential, slower functions like digestion are put on pause. You might suddenly feel sick to your stomach or experience uncontrollable shaking from the shock. Or if you go into a freeze response, you may feel numb and totally shut down. All of this is completely normal to the shock and trauma of betrayal.

Emotionally, the pain, confusion, anger, and sadness feel unbearable. It is hard to know, at times, if it is even possible to survive such intense emotions. I remember standing in the doorframe between our living room and kitchen shortly after life blew up and feeling almost disoriented by the intensity of the pain in my heart, mind, and soul. All I could do at that moment was to focus on one breath at a time. Anything else was too much—too overwhelming. So I breathed in. Then I breathed out. Then I breathed in and out again. As I continued to breathe, the seconds turned into a minute, which turned into an hour, which turned into a day. When the pain threatens to consume you, keep breathing.

Mentally, it is like you can see the shattering happen, and suddenly you find yourself standing in the pile of pieces that was your life—your reality. Eventually, the shock wears off and questions flood your mind:

How could he do this?

Was everything a lie?

Didn't I mean anything to him?

Does this mean our relationship is over?

What else has he done?

Betrayal can shatter your worldview. At first, the devastation of betrayal can make the world seem bad and scary. It's normal to have a heightened sense of fear and mistrust. Your mind is trying to make sense of this new reality you are suddenly forced into. Be very gentle with yourself as you search for your footing.

It can feel unbearable. Hold on.

For a while, you may find yourself numb or bewildered in shock. When reality sets in, though, the emotions come—big, strong, and cycling rapidly. One moment you may feel sad, the next furious, and then hopeless. In one moment you may want him to hold you, and in the next you may never want to see him again.

You are not crazy. This is normal.

It feels torturous—part of you longing for your partner to comfort you, and another part wanting to run away from this person who has hurt you more deeply than perhaps anyone else. You have been suddenly thrown into an impossible situation without warning.[2] Of course you are struggling. This too, unfortunately, is very normal.

You are not crazy.

Another thing you may feel is a profound loss of self-worth. Everyone struggles with insecurities throughout life. Before betrayal, they can be annoying and often come and go. We all know the pain of comparing ourselves to other women, perhaps feeling inadequate as a mom, or wondering what you did wrong when a friend doesn't return your call. But when betrayal hits, it's like every insecurity you've ever had in your life feels confirmed and suddenly on steroids. Every doubt you've ever had about your body, your abilities, your personality, your relationship, and your worth comes roaring back with a vengeance.

Society doesn't help either. Even well-meaning people often default to blaming the betrayed partner. The go-to response is that "she must not have been meeting his needs" or "she must not have been paying enough attention to him." Because many incorrectly believe that "happy men don't cheat."

2. For more information on this internal battle, I recommend reading *The Betrayal Bind: How to Heal When the Person You Love the Most Hurts You the Worst* by Michelle Mays.

That is not true. And those words are so damaging, compounding the feeling of not being good enough, of blaming yourself, and of worthlessness. So let me remind you:

This is not your fault.

You did not cause it.

You have great worth and value.

You are worthy of love and belonging.

You are worthy of truth and faithfulness.

Although you do not deserve betrayal, you are now in a position where you have to deal with it. So let's start with some first steps.

First Steps

The shattering happened. Now what? If you were in an accident and the paramedics arrived on the scene, the first thing they would do is secure the area to ensure no further harm occurs. Next, they would stabilize your vitals. Finally, they would ask you and others for details about what happened. These are important foundational actions, whether responding to an accident or responding to betrayal: Get safe, get help, and get the truth.

Get safe, get help, and get the truth.

Get Safe

Betrayal is overwhelming, and it destroys safety on so many levels. The first step, then, is to get safe. You must have safety to heal. Without safety, there is no healing. Safety comes in many forms—emotional, physical, and psychological—but it doesn't end there. Consider your financial, sexual, and spiritual safety as well.

Identify your most pressing safety needs and focus on those. If you are not sure what they are, then ask yourself the same question my counselor told me to ask: *What do you need to feel safe?* Whatever the answer is, that is your next step. Don't overthink it or talk yourself out of it. Whatever you need to feel safe—do it. Your safety matters. Your wants and needs matter. Your desires matter.

You have the right and the sacred responsibility to hold and protect your broken heart. It's not the time to worry about what others think, and it is not the time to protect your partner. Do what you need to do to stay safe, including the safety of your kids if they are in the house.

You don't have to have everything figured out right away. It's easy to become overwhelmed when thinking of all of the practical and logistical implications, but try not to let those become a barrier to your physical and emotional safety.

It's okay to not be okay.

One of my clients wanted her husband to leave in the wake of the discovery so that she could process her grief, but she felt overwhelmed by the idea of trying to parent on her own. This is a very real and common scenario. In cases like this, I ask my clients to consider what they would need to make it work. Get creative and ask for what you want. Does he need to pick up the kids and take them to school every morning? Do you need to fly Grandma in to help take care of the kids? Do you need to ask a neighbor to bring your son home from soccer after the game? It's okay to ask for help.

It's also okay to not be okay. There is so much pressure to look and act as though you have everything together. This can be for your sake to avoid questions and to save face, for his sake to make things easier for him or to protect his reputation, or for others' sake to prevent them from feeling uncomfortable. I encourage you to be true to yourself and not to focus on others' comfort levels right now. The fact is no one is okay after finding out about betrayal, and that is normal. Allowing yourself to be true to what you need will help the healing process.

Here are some ideas to consider that may be helpful as you brainstorm what you need and what would help you feel safer:

- Connect with a counselor and/or support group.
- Create more space for yourself. This may mean backing out of a volunteer commitment, not signing up to serve at your church, or declining extra projects at work.
- Ask yourself if you feel safe with him in the house or in your bed. If not, ask him to move to the guest bedroom or to go to a hotel. If he refuses, you might decide to go to a hotel or a friend's house.
- Reach out to friends and family to help with meals, transporting kids, and other support that you might need.
- Make sure the house is stocked with food and subscribe to a grocery delivery service (or ask a friend to do so on your behalf) so that you don't have to worry about running out to get milk on top of everything else already on your mind.
- Take a nap or go to bed early so your body can rest.
- Decide whether you want as much information as possible right now or if you want to wait for a full therapeutic disclosure.
- Decide whether you want to process the discovery with your partner present or wait until you can schedule a meeting with a qualified therapist.
- Identify any immediate disclosures that need to be made to kids or other family members. For example, if the FBI is on

their way to the house to pick up a computer, the kids may need an explanation of what is going on.

- For your sexual health and safety, I recommend getting screened for STIs, even if you haven't discovered a physical affair and even if he tells you it's not necessary.

In the coming days and months, you may find yourself needing different things at different times. That is okay. Some days you might be desperate to get out of the house; other days you may not want to get out of bed. Every reaction is normal.

I want to pause and address those who have experienced or are experiencing abuse, coercion, control, and/or domestic violence. Sometimes this is overlooked in the betrayal community, but it is real and devastating. I am sorry if this is part of your story. It is not just you. This is part of many women's stories.

I encourage you, first and foremost, to focus on your safety (and your kids' safety if they are still in the house). Discoveries and/or disclosures often lead to increased violence, so safety must come before everything else, and recovery work or a full disclosure may need to wait until safety is established. If you do not feel safe in your relationship, here are a few things to consider and discuss with your counselor.[3]

- Contact the National Domestic Violence Hotline for help. In the United States, call 800-799-7233 or text BEGIN to 88788.
- Identify a safe place to go, such as a friend's or relative's house or a shelter.

3. Disclaimer: The information provided in this book is for educational purposes only and is not a substitute for professional therapy or safety planning. If you are in immediate danger or experiencing domestic violence, please seek help from a qualified professional who specializes in this area or contact your local emergency services.

- Prepare a "go bag" with essentials such as clothes, medications, documents, money, and keys.
- Make copies of important documents such as birth certificates, marriage certificates, passports, rental agreements, and so on.
- Inform trusted friends and family of the situation.
- If you are ever in imminent danger, call 911 immediately.
- Identify any immediate legal steps that may need to be taken, such as issuing a restraining order, getting a lawyer, or reporting an incident to the police.
- Collect passwords for online banking, email addresses, utilities, cell phone providers, mortgage brokers, and the like.

Your safety is important, and it's not okay for anyone to hurt you for any reason.

Get Help

The next vital step after discovery is to seek help from people who can support you. Healing from betrayal is counterintuitive. Many things you may have been taught about being a good partner no longer work in this situation. If you try to play by the old rules, you may delay, if not stall, the healing process.

It's particularly critical to have help from a qualified counselor or coach who can guide you through the healing process. Unfortunately, most counselors haven't been trained in the complexities and nuances of healing from betrayal. Betrayal is not a general counseling topic; it takes a trained specialist to support you fully. Just as you'd see a cardiologist to get treatment for a heart issue, so too I recommend you see a betrayal specialist to help you heal from intimate betrayal.

Too many times women are deeply hurt by well-meaning counselors, coaches, or pastors who simply don't have expertise in this area. Many counselors view betrayal, infidelity, or sexual addiction as a marital issue, believing both individuals share the blame. That is not the case with betrayal, and it certainly is not a fifty-fifty marriage issue.

The aftermath of betrayal can be very intense. If counselors are not specialized in this area, they may also become overwhelmed and focus on lessening the intensity rather than dealing with the problem—his betrayal. This may come out in several ways, such as not requiring full disclosure, focusing on calming your emotions, vilifying your anger, telling you that you need to forgive and move on, or asking how you contributed to him acting out.

Before you contact a potential counselor, consider what you want out of counseling. This will help determine what counselor is the best fit for you. Here are a few questions to ask yourself:

- What do you want for your relationship right now? Is your goal to stay together no matter what? Are you done and filing papers? Are you not sure yet? There is no right or wrong answer, and your thoughts may change over time, but think through where you are now.
- Are you looking for someone who is gentle and supportive or someone who will provide strong guidance and direction?
- Do you want someone with a faith perspective?

Don't be afraid to interview potential therapists. Ensuring it's a good fit can save you valuable time and money. Here are some questions to ask a potential counselor:

- *Is this an area of specialty for you?* You want someone who specializes in betrayal, not someone who does it on occasion.
- *How did you get into betrayal counseling?* If it's important to you to work with a counselor who has personal experience in this area, this is a good question to ask. If it is their story

and they are open to telling you, you can open the door through this question.

- *What role do you believe a betrayed partner plays in the betrayal?* Their answer will be a major indicator of how the counseling process will unfold. If they imply that you played a role, then I recommend you move on.
- *Do you believe the betrayer can understand why they acted out?* If a counselor says you'll never get the "why" question answered, do not move forward with them. While it's difficult and deep work, your partner can understand his "why." It is also a vital part of his healing and the relationship's ability to heal.
- *What do you believe about full disclosures?* A full disclosure is very important because it gives you the whole truth and ends the secrets. A relationship cannot heal without a foundation of truth, so if a counselor doesn't know what a full disclosure is or doesn't think it's essential, I recommend that you keep looking.

Sometimes, it takes a few tries to find a counselor you connect with and who is the right fit for you. Remember, you're never locked in; you have the freedom to change counselors at any time. Here are a few signs it may be time to move on:

- You are blamed for his betrayal.
- You are asked to do something that feels unsafe, such as having sex with your partner before you are ready.
- The counseling becomes more focused on managing your anger and emotions rather than your partner's need to empathize with those emotions.
- You're pressured to simply forgive or trust and move on.
- Things aren't getting better.

It can be difficult to find the right therapist—especially as many specialists have long waitlists—and it can take a few tries before you find the right person to support you. Stay strong and keep looking.

For those who come from a faith background, it is normal to reach out to your faith leader in times of crisis. I caution you, however, to use discretion when meeting with them. Being a pastor or bishop, for example, does not mean the person is trained in counseling—let alone in handling betrayal issues. In a recent survey, women were asked who they initially talked to about their betrayal. Of family and friends, professional mental health practitioners, or ministry leaders, women found ministry leaders to be the least helpful or even to be hurtful when providing support.[4] So if you hear any of the following, I encourage you to look elsewhere:

- You just need to trust God to heal him.
- You need to submit, forgive, follow his leadership, not get divorced, and so on.
- You need to just love him and be patient.
- He said he was sorry, so you need to forgive him and move forward.
- Married couples are not supposed to deny each other, so you still need to have sex with him.

Of course, most faith leaders are doing their best and want to help, but church hurt is very real. Just because someone is in a position of leadership does not mean they are safe to help you in this area. Trust your gut and remember—as my counselor used to tell me—that your heart is worth protecting.

4. Debra Laaser et al., "Posttraumatic Growth in Relationally Betrayed Women," *Journal of Marital and Family Therapy* 43, no. 3 (February 20, 2017): 435–47.

Get the Truth

Knowing the truth about what your partner has done is important. There are two main ways that the truth comes out: discovery or disclosure. A discovery is when you find something out on your own. You may have discovered a text, walked in on him looking at porn, or been contacted by an affair partner.

A disclosure is different from a discovery.

A disclosure is when your partner offers the information about what he has done. After betrayal, you need a full disclosure, which is when your partner tells you the truth—the whole story. It is his opportunity to come clean and bring his secrets into the light. It is vital if he is going to heal and if the relationship is going to have a chance to heal. These are often most successful when facilitated by a counselor who specializes in betrayal.

You can heal with or without a full disclosure, but it is much easier to heal when you know what you are healing from. Knowing the truth—though painful—allows you to make sense of your relationship and your life, and it allows you to know what you are dealing with. It also gives you the power to make informed decisions about what needs to happen and whether you want to stay in the relationship.

Some betrayed partners do not want a full disclosure for various reasons. You get to decide what is right for you. I highly recommend that your partner still go through the process of writing out the full disclosure for his healing journey, even if you don't want to hear it.

Other forms of getting information include a "drip" disclosure. This is when your partner reveals bits of information over time rather than giving the full truth. It is torturous and can keep you in a perpetual state of being hit with new pain and information.

It also further damages the relationship when you are continually told that you have all the information, only to realize that he lied again. This is how one betrayed partner described going through a drip disclosure:

> It feels like this disclosure process is me sitting silently while he stabs me to death. I feel like it will never end. I so want to trust him and affirm him—and yet he has manipulated me since the moment I met him. I cannot . . . I will not give in. He has to show me he is safe. So much grief. All I can do is hang on . . . hang on for dear life, not knowing if hanging on is simply setting me up for the next crushing attack on my heart . . . an ambush that feels like it will kill me.

Another issue with disclosure is that some betrayed partners only get the truth if they ask the exact right question in the exact right way. This is not a full disclosure and is very damaging as it puts the responsibility for getting the truth on the one who was hurt rather than the one who did the hurting. Trust cannot be rebuilt without the offering of truth. These botched or partial disclosures are incredibly damaging as they continually retraumatize the betrayed partner and further hurt the relationship.

For this reason, it is important to work with a counselor who knows what they are doing when seeking help with the disclosure. A qualified counselor or coach can provide a formal process or structure to follow so that both you and your partner know what to expect throughout the disclosure and so that the full truth is more likely to be revealed.

The format of a full disclosure may differ depending on your counselor's style and training, but at its core it is your partner giving you the complete truth about what he has done. Ideally, it is written out and focuses on the facts and details of his actions without defending, minimizing, blame shifting, or justifying them.

Knowing the Details

You get to decide how much detail you want in the full disclosure. Some betrayed partners want all the details—locations, names, positions, timelines, and so on. They want to understand how it started and how their partner may have lied or gaslit them to hide the truth. Others don't want to hear any of it and just want him to go over the details with his therapist. Many want something in between. There is no right or wrong way. This is a very personal decision. The details you want may also depend on if this is a first disclosure or if you've already endured several.

If you're working with a therapist, make a list of the questions you want answered and share them with your partner and the therapist before the full disclosure so that he can be sure to address them. I also recommend including the question *Is there anything else I should know?*

> *You get to decide how much detail you want in a full disclosure.*

When considering how many details you want, just keep in mind that once you have the details—you have them. You can't unknow the truth once it's revealed. It may cause additional trauma at first and require additional healing. Here's the deal though: You can heal from trauma. I want you to be informed of the risks and benefits of asking for details so you can make an informed decision, but then I encourage you to ask for what you want. This is your opportunity to step into your strength and set a new pattern. Make your choice and go with it.

Joining a support group can be helpful if you're preparing for a full disclosure so that you can hear what questions others have asked and get different opinions on the details you may or may not want to have. It also helps to have people in your corner who understand exactly what you're going through, having walked this path themselves.

Why Do You Need a Full Disclosure?

Many people question whether a full disclosure process is truly necessary. Every experienced betrayal therapist will tell you, "Yes, it is." In an interview I did with Debbie Laaser, MA, LMFT, about the necessity of disclosures, she beautifully captured the reason why the truth is vitally important:

> We're very intuitive people. One of the things that happens when we're living in a relationship where truth is not being told and there are secrets or lies or hiding of some kind, is that our internal reality—what we believe is true—and the external reality—or what we've discovered or have been told by the person that we've been betrayed by—do not match up. And when they don't match up, we have this tension going on between our internal and our external reality that makes us feel crazy.[5]

The way you've experienced your relationship—perhaps as stable, loving, and intimate—no longer aligns with the reality of what you've witnessed or been told about your relationship. There is a mismatch, which causes you to doubt yourself and your instincts. It is this "tension," as Debbie calls it, between what you knew and what you now know. In the aftermath of the discovery, you may still not have the full story. That is where a full disclosure comes in—to fill in the gaps.

Just a reminder: You're not crazy. You aren't stupid or a fool for not seeing it, either. Betrayal does not happen without lying. He

---

5. Debra Laaser, "The Truth, the Whole Truth, and Nothing but the Truth: Full Disclosure for Couples Navigating Relational Betrayal," interview by T. Gustafson, October 12, 2023.

intentionally misled you or fed you a version of reality that was not true. Now he needs to come clean in order to even have a chance at repairing the relationship.

Often, men will not give the full truth without a counselor's help. Your partner needs someone to help him work through his shame, fear, or reluctance that is causing him to hold back information. A counselor can also help provide a great deal of emotional safety for you during this season when a lot of gaslighting[6] and defensiveness can happen.

Finally, a full disclosure is the first step on the long road to rebuilding trust, if he wishes to do so. It's a chance for him to come clean, to give you the gift of truth, and to show you the kind of man that he can be. In our interview, Debbie also stated, "If we're going to build trust, then [it] is about knowing this person will offer us the truth in any situation so that we don't have to be guessing—we don't have to be asking about it." This is about him learning to be vulnerable and transparent with you, to let you into his inner world. Giving you the full truth is the most loving thing he can do for you now.

Waiting

If you decide to work with a therapist and get a full disclosure, there will be a waiting period. Your partner's therapist should work with him to prepare the full disclosure so it is thorough and free of any explanations and blame shifting. How long that takes will vary depending on your partner and the therapist; however, it does not have to take long. In my interview with Dan Drake and Dr. Janice Caudill, coauthors of *Full Disclosure: How to Share the Truth After Sexual Betrayal*, Dan stated that it is possible for the betraying partner to prepare his disclosure in six to eight weeks when he is actively working on it.[7]

---

6. We will talk more about gaslighting later in Phase One.
7. Dan Drake and Janice Caudill, "The Art & Science of Full Disclosures: A Mock Interview," interview by T. Gustafson, November 12, 2024.

This is important to know, especially for professionals, because the wait time is excruciating for betrayed partners. In fact, on a scale of zero to ten, with zero being no pain, betrayed partners rate the initial discovery as 9.6. The pain experienced waiting for a disclosure is 9.2. The pain of disclosure is 7.7.[8] Hearing a full disclosure is less painful than waiting for it.

Unfortunately, the full disclosure process is one where betrayed partners are often disempowered and told they do not have a voice. If you feel that way, I want to empower you that this is your life, your relationship, and your journey. You can speak up and ask questions. You can ask that it be done quickly. You can ask to have a date scheduled. What you want and need is important.

Polygraphs

One tool that helps with full disclosures is a polygraph. It can help confirm whether the betrayer is telling the truth. Many men will reveal more from simply knowing that they are going to do a polygraph.

It is important to know that polygraphs are about 85 percent accurate.[9] It can be discouraging to know they are not foolproof, but they are still a very solid tool in the quest for truth. They are not punishment. They are an opportunity for the betrayer to provide a solid footing to move forward. Most women want their partner to pass. They want to know that the danger is over and that there is a foundation on which to start healing and perhaps even build trust again. After continual lying, a polygraph can be a great way to be fairly sure that you know everything so you can move on from the disclosure process and end what can feel like a continuous emotional beating.

8. Association of Partners of Sex Addicts Trauma Specialists, *APSATS Multidimensional Partner Trauma Model Training, Module 3: Discovery Trauma and Crisis*, and *Module 4: Disclosure Trauma* (published independently, 2019).
9. Stephen Cabler, "Polygraphs 101," interview by T. Gustafson, October 2, 2023.

How do you decide if you need a polygraph? That is a personal decision. Some therapists recommend them, and others do not. This is your life—your relationship—so you get to decide. It is up to you and what you need. You may not want or need your partner to do a polygraph, and that is fine. You may want it done as part of the full disclosure process. You may want it done regularly. There is no right or wrong decision. However, know that if your partner has done a full disclosure and you still have doubts and a gnawing feeling deep inside, then a polygraph is a great option. If you do decide to have your partner take a polygraph, it is very important to find someone who specializes in sexual addiction polygraphs rather than someone who focuses on sexual offenders or forensic polygraphs.

Healing Without the Truth

Sometimes, the one who did the betraying refuses to give a full disclosure or submit to a polygraph. The question for betrayed partners then becomes *Can I still heal without the full truth?* Dr. Jake Porter gave a beautiful response to this question:

> The answer to that is yes, you can. It's going to look different, and it may not be the healing you had hoped for, but you can heal. You have to still grieve, which means you have to assemble a story. [That] means you have to create meaning about what's happened.
>
> If that's my situation—I never got the full disclosure—my story might be, "I'll never know all of my past reality because he continues to not give it to me." That's painful . . . but it's still a story that can set me up to make choices about where to go from here.[10]

Relationships are built on safety and truth. If there is no truth, there is no safety and no solid foundation for trust. A couple may

10. Jake Porter, "Healing Truth: How Disclosure Benefits the Betrayed Brain," interview by T. Gustafson, October 14, 2022.

stay together without the truth, but there cannot be full emotional intimacy and authenticity when he is withholding the truth.

Disclosure Self-Care

The disclosure process can be an incredibly stressful time; the lead-up to it, hearing the truth, and processing through it all is a lot. It is important to be very gentle with yourself. If you are doing a full disclosure with a therapist, I encourage you to consider your options and to create a plan. Here are some questions to consider as you prepare:[11]

- Where do you want the full disclosure to happen? Online? In person? At your therapist's office? At a neutral location, such as an Airbnb? Where do you feel safe?

- If doing it together in person, do you want to drive together or separately?

- Who do you want there?

- Do you want to have a code word or agreement with the therapist if you need to take a time-out during it?

- When do you want it to happen?

- What are some comfort items you can have with you (e.g., blanket, tea, tissues, hard candy, a fidget spinner, comfy slippers)?

- Do you want a copy of his disclosure?

- Do you want him to spend the night at a hotel after the disclosure, or vice versa, so that you have time to process?

11. For more information about your choices and how you can prepare to hear your partner's disclosure, I recommend *Full Disclosure: Seeking Truth After Sexual Betrayal* by Janice Caudill and Dan Drake. It is the companion guide to *Full Disclosure: How to Share the Truth After Sexual Betrayal*, which is for those who did the betraying.

- Do you need him out of your bed, bedroom, or house leading up to and/or after the disclosure?
- If you have kids at home, can someone take care of them and keep them overnight?
- Who is a safe friend you can call after the disclosure for support?

You have choices and get to ask for what you want and need.

Encouragement

Before we move on, let's pause for a moment. This is dark and heavy, so I need you to hear something: You can heal. Believe it or not, it is possible to heal. You will breathe deep again. Not only can you survive, but as you take this one step at a time, you are building strength. You are building skills. In the midst of all the losses, it is possible to make gains as well. Perhaps you stood up for yourself for the first time. Perhaps you are learning to push past your fears and set boundaries for the first time. Perhaps you are finding your voice. It takes so much courage to fight for yourself. Own those gains. Own every ounce of strength you are building and every step you are taking. And keep going.

2

Navigating Emotions

It is normal for emotions to be incredibly intense after finding out about betrayal. You may feel angry, sad, hopeless, disgusted, confused, numb, or even cycle through all of the above. That is to be expected. It is a shock to your body, mind, and emotions. You are suddenly faced with having to rewrite your past and forced to absorb things you never thought possible.

You may feel like you are going crazy because the emotions are so intense and change so quickly. You are not crazy. Full stop. This is normal. One minute you may be curled up in the fetal position and crying on your bathroom floor, and the next you may feel so angry that you want to crawl out of your skin. Even more confusing is the inner battle: One minute you may want to be with your partner and save the relationship, and then the next you may be ready to file for divorce. This is totally normal as well.

The intensity of your emotions may be stronger and last longer than you—or those around you—are comfortable with. Your heart is dealing with the unimaginable, and it needs time to feel its way through everything.

Your journey of healing will, of course, take time. And you get to take as much time as you need. Be patient with yourself. Just as you can't speed up the healing of a broken bone, you can't speed up the healing of your heart. If you were in a major car accident, you would immediately seek professional help at a hospital. You would eat healthy so that your body had the nutrition it needed to recover. You would rest. You would simplify life and ask for help. The ways in which you would care for yourself after a traumatic accident are the same ways you'll want to tenderly care for your heart and soul after betrayal.

> *It is normal for emotions to be*
> *incredibly intense after betrayal.*

Emotional Impact of Betrayal

Pause for a moment and take a breath. You may be feeling overwhelmed with a lot of emotions right now and wondering how you're going to work through them all. I'm going to guide you through a few of the most common emotions and help you understand what's going on in your brain and body from the impact of betrayal.

Pain

The pain of betrayal is overwhelming. It is the doubled-over, not sure if you are going to survive to the next day kind of pain. I see you. I know it hurts. In every way. It is way beyond just mental or emotional pain. It expands to your body and to life itself. I want to offer you hope that it will not always hurt this much. I know that may not bring comfort in this moment, but I offer it as something to hold on to. Keep breathing. Keep going.

Anger

The anger is real. It deserves to be here. A great wrong has been done to you. Don't push it away. You will need the anger to give you strength and courage on this journey. I know it feels scary when it floods your body. I know you, like every betrayed partner, probably have baggage around anger that makes it a difficult, complicated emotion. We will talk more about anger later, but for now, know that your anger is valid and serves a really important purpose on your journey of healing.

Shame

It is common for betrayed partners to feel shame, particularly early on. Shame is "a feeling of being unworthy or disgraced."[1] You may feel shame for what your partner has done or simply for being in a relationship with him or because you fear your partner's actions reflect poorly on you. You may feel shame for staying.

Feeling shame often leads to wanting to hide from people or the world. It is different for everyone, but few make it through the experience of betrayal without this excruciating feeling. Know that you have nothing to be ashamed of. The betrayal was due to his actions, not yours. Knowing that doesn't make the shame go away, but I am going to remind you of that truth.

One of the most effective ways to work through shame is to speak it out loud to safe, trusted people. That is often a safe counselor, coach, friend, or support group. Share what you are feeling ashamed about. Bring it to the light and let it be heard. Shame thrives in the dark and heals in the light. Brené Brown reminds us that "if we can share our story with someone who responds with empathy and understanding, shame can't survive."[2]

1. Urban Dictionary, "shame," accessed March 15, 2025, https://www.urbandic tionary.com/define.php?term=Shame.
2. Brené Brown, *Daring Greatly: How the Courage to Be Vulnerable Transforms the Way We Live, Love, Parent, and Lead* (Gotham Books, 2012), 66.

Fear

It makes sense to feel fear after betrayal: fear of how this will impact everyday life, the kids, his job, your finances, and so on; fear that there's more to the story you don't know; fear that it will happen again. The fears related to the betrayal make sense to us. But you may be surprised that you have fear of things not related to the betrayal and that did not bother you before. Suddenly, being home alone at night may feel scary. You may find yourself driving more defensively in fear of getting in an accident. If your boss is in a bad mood, you may fear for your job though your performance is fine.

These nonrelated fears are common and very understandable for two reasons. First, your brain sends you into fight-or-flight mode when it perceives a threat. You are in survival mode, so you will be more sensitive to other signs of perceived threat. Second, betrayal shakes your worldview. If the person you thought you were safest with is suddenly not safe, it can make you question whether *anything* or *anyone* is safe.

This increased fear usually subsides over time, but in the meantime, there are a couple of things you can do that will help. First, be very gentle with yourself. Do your best not to shame yourself or beat yourself up for feeling fear. Second, remember that reestablishing safety is at the very core of healing. Focus your efforts on things that will make you feel safer. Perhaps you have a friend on the phone as you walk out to your car in the dark after work. Perhaps you install a security camera by your front door or carry pepper spray in your purse. None of this is silly. It is a way to honor and care for yourself.

Loneliness

Even for betrayed partners who are lucky enough to have safe friends, a great counselor, and maybe even a support group, the reality is that at the end of the day you are the only one who can face and work through the betrayal. No one else is having the gru-eling conversations with your partner. Nobody else is with you as you cry yourself to sleep or wake up shaking in the middle of the night. There is nowhere to hide from it. There is nothing anyone can do to fix it, save you, or stop the pain. And that can lead to a profound sense of loneliness.

Although no one can fix the situation or protect you from re-ality, knowing that others care about you and understand what's happening can give you the strength you need for one more day, one more disclosure, one more conversation. That's what you need. You need others in your corner who can breathe life and truth into you and give you the strength you need to go back into the battle.

For those who don't have them yet, I want to let you know that *those people are out there.* There is a world of compassionate, em-powering, caring women who would be honored to welcome you into their loving, supporting, nurturing, healing space—a friend, support group, counselor, or coach—and walk with you. Search them out. Don't give up.

Missing Your Partner

The emotions around betrayal are bewildering, especially in the moments when you feel drawn to the person who hurt you so deeply. Yes, even this is completely normal. There may be times that you want to go back to how it was or pretend—even if for a brief time—that this is not your reality.

There will be times when you miss your partner—or miss the man you thought he was—profoundly. The grief you experience is complicated. It's as though your partner has died, yet he is still there. You may ache for the person you used to feel safe with. You will desperately want him to hold you, want to feel his arms around you. But he is gone. He's not there. In his place is this stranger who has caused you unbearable pain. You now find yourself in a relationship with someone you would have never chosen.

There is an excruciatingly long period when it feels like you are living with a stranger with whom you share everything and nothing, trying to see if this stranger will become the person you thought you knew. It is okay to miss the man you loved.

There is no easy answer or fix for this pain, but I want you to know that I see you and I get it. Keep pressing into healing and into the people who know and love you.

It is okay to miss the man you loved.

Moments of Reprieve

The healing process takes a long time. It is not only okay but healthy to take breaks and allow moments of reprieve when they come. It may be a weekend away with your best friend when you laugh for the first time in a long time. Or getting caught up in a sunset and realizing that, for a moment, you could forget about all the pain and just experience peace.

If you are still with your partner, there may also be moments when you feel safe enough to cuddle or you find yourself smiling at an inside joke. It doesn't mean that everything is okay, and you can verbalize that, but it is okay to allow yourself to enjoy those moments. The fight will be waiting for you on the other side. It's okay to allow your heart—and your nervous system—these moments of reprieve.

Let's pause.

We've just covered a lot of deep and painful realities, so I want to take a moment and remind you of a few truths.

53

You can heal.

You have great worth and value.

You are worthy of love and kindness.

What you want and need matters.

It is possible to come out of this a stronger, more complete version of yourself.

You don't have to believe me. I will hold it until you can hold it for yourself.

Understanding the Impact of Trauma

Because betrayal wreaks such havoc on the body, mind, and emotions, it makes sense that so many betrayed partners feel confused, scared, and out of control. That is a normal response to trauma, and since betrayal is a traumatic event for most, let's get clear on what it is. First of all, at its core, trauma is an event that overwhelms our brain's capacity to process. It is too much, too fast, too painful, or too shocking. It impacts all aspects of life, including mental, emotional, and physical.

Betrayal is a traumatic event for most.

Mental Impact

When a traumatic experience occurs, it is fragmented in the brain and so doesn't get processed the same way as a normal experience. Essentially, it gets stuck. These are the memories you try to avoid or that make you cringe when you touch them. The problem is they don't die or go away. Trauma, like grief, does not heal on its own with time. It is very patient and will hang out indefinitely until you are ready to face and heal it. In the meantime, it remains trapped in the body and festers. Bessel

54

van der Kolk, author of *The Body Keeps the Score*, puts it this way: "Trauma is not just an event that took place sometime in the past; it is also the imprint left by that experience on mind, brain, and body."[3]

Trapped trauma may be patient, but it is not silent. It shifts the way we view life, the world, others, and ourselves. Then it drives our beliefs and behaviors in ways we may not be aware of. Van der Kolk goes on to say, "Trauma causes people to remain stuck in interpreting the present in light of an unchanging past."[4]

Emotional Impact

Emotions are body-based. If you are anxious, you feel tightness in your chest. If you are upset, your stomach might churn. If you are scared, your muscles tense. After betrayal, the emotions can feel unbearably intense, and many betrayed partners unconsciously disconnect with their body in an attempt to bury the emotions and manage the unmanageable. To borrow a saying often attributed to Thomas Edison, it can feel like "the chief function of the body is to carry the brain around." It is understandable to experience the relationship between your body and brain in that way; however, this mindset hinders healing.

The problem is when you bury emotions, you bury them alive. They don't die or go away. You also cannot pick and choose what emotions you disconnect from. If you disconnect from the difficult emotions of fear, anger, and powerlessness, you also disconnect from joy, peace, and contentment.

When you bury emotions, you bury them alive.

---

3. Bessel van der Kolk, *The Body Keeps the Score: Brain, Mind, and Body in the Healing of Trauma* (Penguin Books, 2014), 21.
4. Van der Kolk, *The Body Keeps the Score*, 307.

Physical Impact

Trauma has a very strong impact on the body. Adrenaline and cortisol—powerful stress hormones—flood our system, enabling us to fight, flee, freeze, or fawn. The problem is that those stress hormones don't simply disappear when the threat has passed. They flow through our bloodstream in a constant cycle, ready to spike again at any moment because when you've experienced trauma, you never want to be caught unaware again. Whether or not you are consciously aware of it, your body is primed for another attack.

If left unchecked, this can impact your health. In my HAB survey of betrayed partners, 64 percent reported being diagnosed with a major medical condition since learning of their partner's betrayal. The most common diagnoses included gastrointestinal (29 percent), autoimmune (21 percent), heart issues (20 percent), migraines (15 percent), and chronic fatigue (15 percent). The majority (71 percent) of those diagnoses were received within two years after learning about the betrayal.

Reconnecting with your body and taking care of it is core to healing and empowerment, so start small and just notice it. Notice when your body is tense. Notice when it is calm. Notice where you feel the emotions. Speak kindly and lovingly to it. Your body is working so hard and doing its best to take care of you. Rest when you are tired. Eat when you are hungry. I know our relationship with our body is very complicated after betrayal, but I want to plant the seed that you and your body are on the same team and it is possible to heal. Here's the powerful truth: By giving compassionate attention to your body, you can prevent or alleviate so many of the potential negative impacts that trauma can have. You have power.

Betrayal Trauma

The term "betrayal trauma" is now widely accepted in the United States. It speaks to the impact and devastation a betrayed partner experiences. The idea that betrayed partners are experiencing trauma was a helpful move from the previous lens of seeing people who have been betrayed as codependent or co-addicts. Dr. Barbara Steffens was at the forefront of this shift, and it gave a more compassionate lens for understanding the experiences and reactions of betrayed partners.

I am very grateful for the shift in how betrayed partners are viewed. And I have to be honest that I did not resonate with this term when life blew up for me. The idea that I had to deal with his betrayal and my betrayal trauma felt overwhelming.

I say that to offer space for those who may hear the term "betrayal trauma" and feel it is not a weight they can or want to bear. If that term offers validation, hold on to it. If not, let it go. Either way, keep moving and focus on your healing.

Healing Trauma

Trauma is a wound, but the beautiful thing is that we are designed to heal. Think about it from a physical perspective. If you get a cut—as long as it does not become infected—your body will naturally move toward healing. The same is true psychologically. There is a natural drive toward healing there as well. Those painful trauma memories keep finding ways to come up—not to torment you but to push you toward healing.

To heal the trauma of betrayal, you must face it. When you face it, you feel it. It takes courage to feel what you worked so hard to not feel. But there is freedom and peace on the other side. When you are ready to take that brave step, there are several effective ways to heal trauma, including modalities such as Eye Movement Desensitization and Reprocessing (EMDR) and Somatic Experiencing.[5]

5. For more information on Somatic Experiencing, I recommend Dr. Peter Levine's book *In an Unspoken Voice: How the Body Releases Trauma and Restores Goodness*.

Calming Practices

As you're feeling the impact of betrayal, I want to introduce you to four body-based practices that help activate the parasympathetic nervous system, the system that sends the "all safe" message to your body so the stress hormones can return to baseline levels. Finding specific things that calm your nervous system is critically important for both your short- and long-term healing.

Breathe

Navy SEALs are trained to plunge into dangerous situations; they are held to the highest standards of courage, honor, and discipline so that they can face any fear without backing down. So it might surprise you to learn that along with skills such as how to use weapons, fight in hand-to-hand combat, or endure extreme weather conditions, Navy SEALs learn to *breathe.*

Navy SEALs are taught a breathing method called "box breathing," also known as square breathing, which helps them to clear their minds, slow their heart rate, and stay calm amid danger.[6] This is an effective way to calm your body when it is activated. I encourage you to try this out the next time you are triggered or overwhelmed by emotion. Here's how to do it: Slowly inhale for four counts. Hold your breath for four counts. Exhale for another four counts. Then pause for four counts. Continue repeating this cycle for five minutes.

Move

Movement is one of the best ways to reconnect with yourself and activate your body's natural healing instincts. Movement releases endorphins, activates different parts of the brain, strengthens muscles,

6. Mark Divine, "The Breathing Technique a Navy SEAL Uses to Stay Calm and Focused," *TIME*, May 4, 2016, https://time.com/4316151/breathing-technique-navy-seal-calm-focused.

and bolsters the immune system. Walking—one of the simplest and most basic forms of movement we can practice—mimics the bilateral stimulation of EMDR therapy. Bilateral stimulation is calming to the amygdala (the fear/alert center) of your brain. Movement is therapeutic. It doesn't matter how you decide to move: Walk, swim, bike, run, dance, practice yoga, or go to that Pilates class your friend has been inviting you to. The goal is to get out and move.

Write

Writing by hand is another healing practice. It lets you express your emotions on the page and allows you to vent when no one is there to listen or when it is not safe to say things out loud. It can also help you put the pieces together and try to make sense of your story of betrayal.

Dr. James Pennebaker studied the effects of what he calls "expressive writing" on health and found enormous evidence of writing's healing power as it helps to make meaning, find explanations, and close open loops in the mind. In an article for *The New York Times*, Emily Esfahani Smith, author of *The Power of Meaning*, writes, "In Dr. Pennebaker's research, the people who reported the greatest health and well-being gains initially had disjointed and raw stories, but their narratives became more coherent and insightful as the days went on. Expressive writing helped them to come to a new understanding of the event and how it affected their lives—to tell a story about their suffering."[7]

Touch

We experience the world through our senses, and sometimes the most powerful way to reassure our bodies that we are safe and can return to a state of stability is through our sense of touch. Touch

7. Emily Esfahani Smith, "We Want to Travel and Party. Hold That Thought," *New York Times*, June 24, 2021, https://www.nytimes.com/2021/06/24/opinion/covid -pandemic-grief.html.

helps decrease levels of stress hormones and instead increases oxytocin—the bonding hormone that helps us build relationships. Touch has been shown to decrease pain and improve circulation. It also helps to calm our nervous system.

Touch may feel complicated after betrayal. On the one hand, you may crave physical contact with your partner, while on the other hand, it may feel repulsive. There are other ways to find comfort in touch, though, that don't involve your partner if you don't want it to. If touch sounds safe and possibly comforting to you or if you want to experiment with it, then here are some recommendations:

- Hug a safe friend or family member.
- Pet an animal.
- Use a weighted blanket.
- Experiment with different temperatures and tastes. A soothing cup of tea might be exactly what you need—or a refreshing iced coffee instead.
- Take a bath or soak your feet.
- Get a massage, facial, manicure, or pedicure.
- Get your hair done and ask for a scalp massage.
- Try applying a cooling gel face mask or warming up a heat compress for your lower back.

The key is to connect with what you want and need and to honor that.

Reconnecting with your body and taking care of it is core to healing and empowerment.

3

Interacting with Your Partner

Interacting with your partner during Phase One when you are still dealing with the shock and trying to get the truth is very difficult and painful. You may not even recognize the man in front of you, let alone want to look at him. In this chapter, I will help you navigate this new territory and give you tools for interacting with him.

During this phase, your partner may or may not have even left the starting block of healing. His secrets, at least in part, are out but not yet fully revealed. The betrayer is often deep in shame and may be cycling through relief, regret, and anger. He may still be defensive, unable to take your anger or show you empathy. If he is preparing for a full disclosure, his stress and resistance may be high.

If any of that rings true for you, then your focus on interacting with your partner during this phase needs to be strongly focused on protecting yourself. There are three things to focus on to help keep you safe during this volatile time: healthy detachment, boundaries, and understanding gaslighting.

Healthy Detachment

Healthy detachment is an important tool for protecting yourself and regaining your footing after betrayal. The best description of detachment I've heard came from a member of one of my support groups. She said, "To me, detachment is turning my attention and energy from him to what I need and taking care of myself rather than looking to him to take care of me. I don't have to wait for him to meet my need. I can meet it myself." It creates an emotional buffer between you and him. Healthy detachment is not disconnecting, and it doesn't necessarily mean that you are out of the relationship, but it gives you a chance to catch your breath and begin to heal. There is an aspect of empowerment and a deep sense of caring for yourself—no longer waiting for him to meet your needs. Essentially, healthy detachment creates space and makes you *more available* to yourself and *alive* to the world around you.

"Detachment is turning my attention and energy from him to what I need and taking care of myself rather than looking to him to take care of me."

Start by identifying your needs. These may include safety, love, companionship, empathy, fun, comfort, and so on. Once you've made your list, then ask yourself how you can meet those needs for yourself. It may mean taking steps to get there. Perhaps to be able to provide for yourself financially, you first need to finish your degree, update your résumé, or study for a new certification at work. Perhaps you need to start shifting how you talk to yourself to give yourself love and acceptance. Maybe you need to brush off an old hobby that you have abandoned—or find a new one—so that you can enjoy fun and laughter again. Healthy detachment allows you to take responsibility for your healing and safety regardless of what your partner may choose.

Boundaries

When life blew up, Hannah[1] felt like she no longer knew who she was. Her role as a wife was foundational to her identity. With her marriage now hanging by a thread, she had no idea who she would be if it ended. She was terrified to consider the possibility of a future where the perceived safety and security she felt in that position were gone. Without her husband, she wondered, *Who am I?* She felt completely adrift and alone, lost in a sea of sadness. She knew, though, that if she was going to be okay again, she would have to figure out how to navigate life on her own. She would have to set boundaries and find a sense of stability that came from within herself rather than be dependent on the person she had always relied on but no longer could.

Hannah felt guilty trying to find her footing. She grew up in a faith culture where she was taught not to focus on herself or think too highly of herself and to put others first. It was implied that boundaries were bad and that focusing on her own needs and desires was selfish.

Hannah remembered journaling one day and realizing that all of the messages she had received growing up—all of the "shoulds" she had absorbed throughout her life—were now holding her back from the healing she knew needed to happen. She had to decide that what she thought, felt, and wanted was important. She had to make the choice to see that she could show up in her life.

As we discuss the important topic of boundaries, I want to acknowledge that this is difficult. Like Hannah, you may feel uncomfortable if you are not used to focusing on yourself and what

1. The person's name and identifying details have been changed or presented in composite form to ensure privacy, safety, and anonymity.

you need. But boundaries are key to stepping into your power and healing after betrayal. The reality is your wants and needs are important. You deserve happiness and respect. You get to take up space in this world.

Now, let's dive into boundaries. Henry Cloud and John Townsend describe them well: "Boundaries define us. They define what is me and what is not me. A boundary shows me where I end and someone else begins, leading me to a sense of ownership."[2] The act of setting boundaries involves putting your wants and needs into words.

Boundaries often have a lot of baggage associated with them—particularly messages received in childhood. I encourage you to take some time and make a list of what you were told or what you came to believe about boundaries. Many women were given the message that boundaries are bad, mean, punishing, selfish, or just don't work. Others may have been lucky enough to grow up in a home where boundaries were honored and respected. No matter your starting point, I want to offer perhaps a different way of looking at boundaries.

Let's take a step outside of the betrayal world for a moment and notice boundaries in the physical world. Roads have lines to keep cars in their respective lanes. Countries have boundary lines. Fences divide your backyard from your neighbor's. Even your skin is a type of boundary that separates you from the world around you. Boundaries are a natural and necessary part of life—keeping the world from falling into chaos.

The same is true in our relationships and emotional world. You get to decide how you want things to operate with your physical body and in your internal world. You get to communicate what you are okay with and what you are not okay with. You get to choose how you interact or don't interact with others. You get to ask people

2. Henry Cloud and John Townsend, *Boundaries: When to Say Yes, How to Say No to Take Control of Your Life*, updated and expanded edition (Zondervan, 2017), 29.

to leave if you choose, and if they don't, you can. Your space and peace are worth protecting, and boundaries can help you do that.

Boundaries define where you end
and another person begins.

Defining Your Personal Circle

The first step in your journey of setting healthy, empowered boundaries is to define what I call your personal circle.

To understand the idea of your personal circle, I invite you to put your arms out in front of you and touch your fingers—as if you were hugging a tree. This is your personal circle. It represents you. In it is everything that makes you *you*: your likes and dislikes, your history, traumas, successes, personality, fears, interests, dreams, desires, and so on. The outside of your arms represents where you end and where others begin. Each person has their own personal circle filled with everything that makes them who they are.

SELF
Favorite Things
Wounds   Dreams
Emotions   Wants / Needs
Experiences   Reactions
Successes / Failures
. . . everything you

Start by identifying what is in your circle. Make a list of the things that make you who you are. Write down everything that comes to mind, and remember, there are no wrong answers. Don't worry if it's hard to figure this out in the beginning. Just come back to it over time and add things to your list as you think of them.

If you get stuck or are struggling with this exercise, talk to people who know and love you to get ideas. Ask them to tell you what they love about you—maybe their favorite memory of you or a story about you as a child. Sometimes it is helpful to get outside perspectives, but always go back to your own personal reflection and make sure their answers feel true to you.

Another good way to gain insight into yourself is to take a personality test. There are several options, including Myers-Briggs, the Enneagram, and the Big 5 personality survey, to name a few. The results of these tests do not define who you are, but they can provide valuable insights.

Taking Responsibility for What's in Your Circle

Once you have identified what's in your circle—what makes you *you*—the second step is to take responsibility for everything in that circle. It's yours to own, nurture, and care for. Celebrate those parts of you that you are proud of. Compassionately care for the parts that are hurting or need healing. If there are parts that have been neglected or need attention, then it is your job to nurture them. Your job is to own and care for your circle.

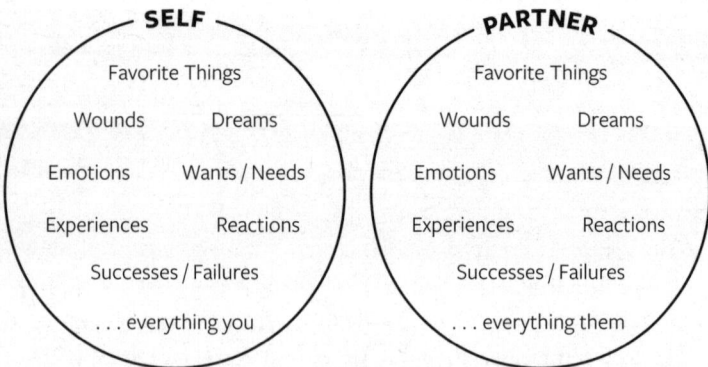

SELF

Favorite Things

Wounds   Dreams

Emotions   Wants / Needs

Experiences   Reactions

Successes / Failures

. . . everything you

PARTNER

Favorite Things

Wounds   Dreams

Emotions   Wants / Needs

Experiences   Reactions

Successes / Failures

. . . everything them

Recognizing What's Not in Your Circle

The third and final step is to recognize what doesn't belong in your circle. Again, everyone has their own circle. As illustrated at the bottom of page 66, your partner has his own circle, and he is responsible for his actions, emotions, and reactions to you. You are not responsible for what is in his circle.

Here's the thing about personal circles though: Few women are taught about them. Few women know who they are, know how to nurture what is in their circle, or are taught that they get to take up space in life. As a result, one of two things often happens. For most, our arms are wide open rather than closed in a circle. When this happens, it is not clear where one person ends and the other begins. Other people's stuff gets pushed onto you, and your stuff gets pushed onto others . . . and it is all one big, jumbled mess. There is no sense of self, no ownership of what is yours, and no clear understanding of what is not yours.

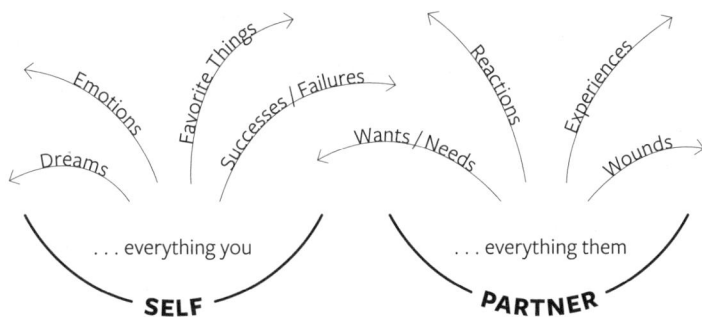

Emotions   Favorite Things   Successes / Failures   Dreams   Wants / Needs   Reactions   Experiences   Wounds

. . . everything you   **SELF**

. . . everything them   **PARTNER**

If this is you, there is no shame or judgment. Your challenge though is to close your circle so that you are clear about who you are and empowered to take ownership of your life.

The other common scenario is that you may have a personal circle but it is very small. This is common with women who were told early on that they needed to be small or invisible, that they were too much, or that what they wanted in life didn't matter. As

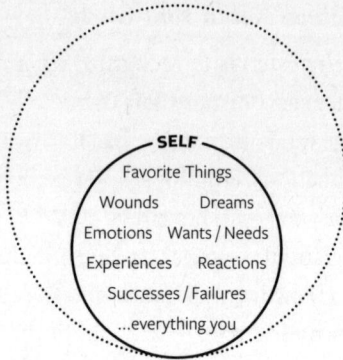

a result, they became small and tried to stay out of everyone's way and not upset anybody. If you resonate with this circle, I want to encourage you: *You get to take up space in this world.* You are important. You were never meant to be small or invisible. Your wants, needs, and desires matter. You get to use your voice and express yourself. You get to step into the space you were designed to fill.

You get to take up space in this world.

Responding by Using Your Circle

Now that you have your circle, you may be wondering what it has to do with boundaries. Here's the power of the personal circle: When something happens in life or with your partner, you get to press pause and take a mental—or perhaps physical—time-out to go back to your personal circle to ground and reconnect with yourself. As you do that, ask yourself three questions:

1. *What happened?*
2. *How do I feel about it?*
3. *What do I need to feel safe?*

68

As an example, let's say you were talking with your partner about his betrayal, and he got angry and gaslit you. Perhaps he blame shifted, saying that if you would have had more sex with him, he wouldn't have acted out. When you are hit with something like that, you get to pause and take a time-out.

First, ask yourself what just happened. *My partner just blamed his acting out on me rather than taking responsibility and ownership for it.*

Second, ask yourself how you feel about it. You may think, *I'm angry. We did have sex, and even if it wasn't as often as he wanted, that doesn't mean it was my fault he cheated on me. That was his decision.*

Finally, ask yourself what you need to feel safe. You may think, *To feel safe, I need some time away from him. I don't want him sleeping in bed with me tonight since he does not know how much he hurt me. I want him to sleep on the couch. Or if he won't, then I will.*

Then you verbalize to him what you need to feel safe. By doing this, you are naturally setting a boundary that flows from inside you. Standing firm inside of your personal circle and staying in touch with yourself and your needs is powerful and empowering. It allows you to stay grounded and—in this case—to resist his gaslighting and know what you need to feel safe. It is a vital part of the healing process and a step toward feeling more empowered.

You were never meant to be small or invisible.

Learning how to set healthy boundaries is like learning any new skill; it may take some time and effort, but you can do it. Remember to be very gentle with yourself. The reality is most betrayed partners struggle with boundaries in the beginning. However, when women lean into this work, an inner strength starts to grow. They start to believe in themselves. They learn to own what is theirs and connect with themselves. They use their voice and take up space. This work has the potential to not only create strong, healthy shifts in your relationship but also cultivate your sense of well-being, strength, and direction.

Understanding Gaslighting

Gaslighting is, unfortunately, a very common dynamic with betrayal. Let's focus on understanding what it is, recognizing it, learning how to respond to it, and healing from it.

What Is Gaslighting?

The term "gaslighting" comes from the 1944 film *Gaslight* in which a man tries to convince his partner that she is crazy so he can steal the family jewels, which she doesn't realize are in the attic of their house. Every time he goes to the attic and turns on the light to search, it dims the rest of the lights in the house. To cover up what he is doing, he engages in several tactics to make her question her reality.

Gaslighting can be defined as "the effort of one person to undermine another person's confidence and stability by causing the victim to doubt [their] own sense and beliefs."[3] Another way to define it is "systematically withholding factual information from, and/or providing false information to, the victim—having the gradual effect of making them anxious, confused, and less able to trust their own memory and perception."[4] Can you relate?

Gaslighting makes you doubt your reality and shifts the focus off your partner and onto you. And if he can get you to buy into

3. Neal A. Kline, "Revisiting Once Upon a Time," *American Journal of Psychiatry* 163, no. 7 (July 2006): 1147–48.
4. Urban Dictionary, "gaslighting," accessed March 15, 2025, https://www.urbandictionary.com/define.php?term=Gaslighting.

the idea that somehow the issue is your fault, then he is off the hook.

Gaslighting comes in many forms, including excuses, justifications, unfair questions, and outright denials of the truth. It may sound something like the following:

- "We weren't having sex enough, so it's your fault."
- "You were ignoring me after the baby was born, and I had to get my needs met."
- "Why are you still angry? Why aren't you over it?"
- "It's just porn . . . at least I didn't sleep with someone. It's not that bad."

In each of these instances, he refuses to take ownership of what he did and instead makes it your fault and your responsibility. Gaslighting can include but is not limited to the following:

- Blame shifting
- Lying, by what he says or what he doesn't say (i.e., lies of omission)
- Denying
- Attacking (e.g., "You're crazy!")
- Projecting
- Rationalizing
- Minimizing

Most women I've worked with genuinely care about their partner. As a result, they often take his words at face value—which is exactly what he's counting on. She may wonder, *Am I a bad person? Why can't I get myself together? Why can't I heal faster? Am I being unreasonable? Is this my fault?* Gaslighting makes her doubt herself and take responsibility for things that are not hers to own.

Dr. Jennifer Freyd developed the concept known as DARVO, which stands for Deny, Attack, and Reverse Victim and Offender roles. DARVO is similar to gaslighting and is a powerful weapon used against betrayed partners. Dr. Freyd explains:

> DARVO is a defensive strategy that a person who's been accused of something—such as sexual infidelity—can use so that person can deny (D) that he did the act at all. [Then he] can attack the true victim in the situation, typically attacking (A) their credibility in some way, like, *You're just saying this because you want to manipulate me or your memory is poor or you were drunk.* And then the really insidious part is reversing victim and offender (RVO). The unfaithful spouse says, *You are harming me with your false accusation. You're trying to control me. You're trying to ruin my reputation. You're doing this terrible thing to me.* And putting the person who raises the problem into the role of the offender.[5]

Gaslighting can happen intentionally or unintentionally. Sometimes, men will intentionally gaslight their partners to control and manipulate them. If your partner is purposely manipulating you and controlling you, that's a serious problem. That's a deeper issue, and you are not safe in that relationship. You're going to need help as you determine how to respond.

Many betrayers, however, gaslight their partners in an effort to avoid discomfort and responsibility. Their attitude is unintentionally, *I don't want to talk about this. I don't want to deal with this right now.* It's their defense mechanism, a way of putting up a shield and deflecting the questions and accountability coming at them.

Here's the thing though: Whether he is gaslighting you intentionally or unintentionally, the result is the same. You start to question

5. Jennifer Freyd, "Understanding Betrayal Blindness & DARVO," interview by T. Gustafson, October 31, 2024.

yourself and your reality. Either way, it is harmful and detrimental to you.

How to Recognize Gaslighting

Where there is intimate betrayal, there is usually gaslighting, so it is important to know how to recognize it when it happens. Now that you've read some examples of gaslighting, think of a time when your partner gaslit you and try to put yourself back in that situation. What did you feel in your body? Was your heart racing? Did your chest tighten? Did things start to feel foggy?

What thoughts were going through your mind? Maybe you thought, *Oh my gosh, I'm going crazy;* or *I'm so confused;* or *Here we go again.*

What emotions did you feel? Hopeless? Sad? Angry? Perhaps you felt like there was nothing you could do.

When have you felt this way before? My guess is that you've probably felt these same things at other times. My goal is to help you recognize the pattern of what you experienced so that you can catch it in future situations.

Recognizing the pattern of how you feel in your body is the fastest and most effective way to know when you are being gaslit. Your body will be the first to tell you it is happening because the goal of gaslighting is to mentally confuse you and make you question yourself and your reality. But your body tells the truth, and when you recognize the pattern in your body, trust it.

As with all the skills you're learning, be gentle with yourself as you learn to trust your body and recognize gaslighting. It is a gradual process. At first, recognition will be slow. You'll find yourself ruminating over a conversation the next day, and suddenly you'll realize that you were being gaslit. And then you'll get to the point where, a few hours later, you'll think, *Wait a second, I wasn't crazy!* And then, as time goes on, you'll realize what's happening at the end of the argument . . . and then eventually in the middle of the argument. This is a process of recognition. Every time you do recognize it, no matter how long it took, that's a win.

One of the great things about recognizing the feeling of gaslighting in your body is that you are looking to yourself and reaffirming that you can trust the signals you're receiving from your body, mind, and heart. You're saying, *I can trust myself. I know that feeling in my body and I can trust it.* This is part of the beautiful, empowering journey of healing your relationship with yourself.

Learn to recognize the feeling of being gaslit in your body.

How to Respond to Gaslighting

It's one thing to recognize that your partner is gaslighting you, but then what do you do? It is so easy to get sucked into an argument, defending yourself and trying to get him to understand your point of view. The argument often escalates from there, sending you spiraling. It is incredibly frustrating, and it can feel like you are beating your head against the wall and getting nowhere.

Here's the thing: Once your partner is in gaslighting mode, you will not be able to reach him or reason with him. He will rarely shift out of it within the conversation. He is most likely locked down. It is important to know this because it will be very natural for you to want to get through to your partner and get him to understand your point of view. Now is not the time. Your best bet is to end the conversation and come back to it when he is no longer in gaslighting mode.

Of course, ending the conversation is so much easier said than done. Gaslighting is intended to hook you, and that hook is very powerful. I want to offer a way out, with the understanding that everyone gets sucked in at times and perfection is not the goal.

But I want you to have this knowledge, as it will save you a lot of pain, anger, and frustration. It is also another way to take care of yourself.

First, similar to the boundary-setting process, take a time-out. This might be a literal time-out, where you leave the room and take a moment to collect yourself. It could also be an internal, mental pause. Imagine a hood coming down over your head or an invisible force field around you. Then ask yourself, *What just happened?* Reflecting on his words, you might think, *Okay, he just told me that I am controlling because I asked him to call me if he is going to get home late after work.*

Then go back to your personal circle and ask yourself if what he said is true. Remember, the goal is to take responsibility for what is yours and not take responsibility for what is his. You may look inside and conclude, *No, I'm not being controlling. He used to act out after work, so it does not feel safe when he gets home late without calling me. I am asking for something that will help me feel safe, which is reasonable and healthy. I need safety. He is gaslighting and shifting blame onto me.*[6]

After you are more clear on what is going on and what is yours—and not yours—then name it and redirect him. This might sound like, "You are gaslighting me right now. This is your issue, not mine. You need to figure this out with your counselor." By naming what's going on, you're reaffirming your trust in yourself. *You* get to dictate your reality, not him. In this response, you are also firmly maintaining the integrity of your personal circle.

Finally, as I mentioned before, do your best to end the conversation. He'll likely want to argue, but no good will come of it. By ending the conversation, you are enforcing a boundary and keeping

---

6. This takes a level of strength and clarity that is sometimes hard to come by alone. It can be very helpful to get an outside perspective from someone you trust to help you see it clearly. Talking through scenarios with a counselor or support group can also be very helpful as you grow in this area.

yourself safe. You can come back at another time and address concerns that either of you might have, but nothing productive will happen when he is in gaslighting mode.

There is one big exception to how I suggested you respond to gaslighting, and that is if your partner is abusive, is violent, has threatened violence, or is otherwise unsafe. In that case, confronting him and setting boundaries may put you in more danger. Safety always comes first. If you are in that situation, then there is a whole separate issue of abuse at play. I recommend you pause reading this book and connect with a counselor who is experienced in helping women with domestic violence—even if your partner has not hit you—to determine your next steps.

How to Heal from Gaslighting

It is important to be intentional in healing from gaslighting so that you can regain your clarity and sense of reality. At the core, that involves creating space for yourself, taking space *from* the one who is gaslighting you, and grounding yourself so you can take your power back.

Consider taking time away. It is very difficult to get your feet back under you when your reality continues to be attacked and questioned. Do you need to go away for a weekend? Do you need to ask him to move out of the bedroom so you have a safe space at home? Is it to the point that he needs to move out for a few months—or permanently? Consider what you want and need. The goal is for you to have space to get your feet back under you, to allow your nervous system time to calm, and to get recentered in your reality.

As you heal, you will need other voices who can speak truth and health to you. This will help you regain a sense of what is true, particularly about who you are. If your partner keeps telling you that you are a selfish, controlling person, over time, you may come to believe that. By spending time with other healthy people who know you, they can reflect back on you the truth of who you are and what is happening.

One of the tragedies of gaslighting is that you can lose yourself. Reclaiming yourself is at the core of healing from gaslighting. While it is very important to connect with and get feedback from others, ultimately, you want to know and connect with yourself. That can start by turning your focus to yourself with love and compassion. That may include simply noticing your body and how it feels. Consider journaling to connect with your thoughts and feelings. Do something that you enjoy—or used to enjoy—and reconnect with that feeling of fun and of prioritizing yourself. This is a journey, so start small and make conscious decisions to move toward reconnecting with yourself.

Sex

One of the most difficult interactions to navigate with your partner in Phase One—and beyond—is sex. At this point, you still may not have the full truth about what he has done. Your mind may be filled with images of him acting out, and the very idea of having sex may be repulsive to you. Or you may want to have sex even more as a way to feel close when everything seems to be falling apart around you. There is no right and wrong. There are no rules you need to follow. The only thing that matters here is what is right and safe for you. You get to decide, and what you want may change over time.

First, you need to know that you have ownership of your body and you get to decide what you want to do or don't want to do. He does not get to make that decision for you. Not anymore. You do not owe him anything. If before you felt obligated to have sex with him, his betrayal shattered that pattern. You now get to make the decisions about sex and your body that feel right to you. If you do not want to have sex, you don't have to. You can say no. You have choices.

Some betrayed partners have an increased sexual drive after finding out about the betrayal. Again, it is your body, and you get to make choices about what you want to do. I will give a gentle word of caution though. It's not uncommon for betrayed partners to try to save the relationship by being more sexual after a discovery or disclosure. Many think that if they have more sex, dress sexier, or agree to try the position they previously refused to do, then perhaps he won't act out again. This can result in you crossing lines that you would not otherwise be comfortable doing. Your body, comfort, and safety are important. You don't have to change anything about yourself to be worthy of respect and faithfulness. You don't need to compromise your safety. You are already worthy of love exactly as you are.

Many clients have told me that they feel like they prostituted their body to their partner in order to try to save the relationship. By doing so, they feel that they betrayed themselves. If you resonate with that, I offer so much compassion. You are not alone and there is no shame or judgment. I encourage you to be gentle with yourself, and I offer the idea of extending compassion to that part of you who was trying her best. It is tempting to shame that part of you or banish it. Instead, that part needs love and acceptance. That is one of the deep keys to healing yourself through all of this—loving and accepting yourself, even the complicated and messy parts.

As a reminder, no matter what he—or society—tells you, his betrayal is never your fault. It was not a result of what you did or did not do sexually, how often you had sex, what your body looks like, or what positions you would or would not participate in. *His* betrayal stemmed from *his* deeper issues that he had not dealt with. You did not cause it and unfortunately you don't have the power to prevent it. Only he can make that choice.

You get to decide if you want to have
sex with your partner or not.

One topic that is sensitive but needs to be addressed is the fact that sexual abuse is a reality in many relationships. In fact, in the HAB survey, over 32 percent of betrayed partners said that they experienced some form of sexual abuse in their relationship, including one or more of the following: unwanted touching, coerced sex, rape, or sexual assault. Just as anyone would say that it's never okay for a stranger to do any of these things to you, neither is it okay for your partner to do any of them to you—ever. Sexual abuse is sexual abuse, no matter what your relationship is with that person. You do not deserve any of it, and I recommend you seek professional support if you have experienced sexual abuse.

Potential Stuck Points

Just as there are things that are important to focus on during Phase One, there are also things to not focus on because they will stall your healing process. The four things *not* to focus on include forgiveness, trust, your partner's emotions, and your "stuff."

Forgiveness

Phase One is not the time to focus on forgiveness. It is important and there is a time for it, but not right now. It is too soon. You are still working through the shock and intense emotions and trying to get to the truth. Forgiveness comes later. It comes on the other side of anger. It comes on the other side of knowing what you need to forgive. It comes on the other side of feeling and wrestling with all the pain and grief of a shattered past, lost years, and an unsure future. If you focus on forgiveness too early, your healing process will shut down. You will miss the process of getting to the truth and working through the betrayal's profound impact.

The temptation in Phase One is to want to forgive in the hope that it will make the pain stop or speed up the healing process. Many believe that if they can just forgive, it will wipe away all that has happened, helping them to move on more quickly. Unfortunately, that doesn't work.

Depending on your background and if you grew up in a faith tradition, there can also be a lot of pressure to forgive right away. The message is that you must forgive immediately and move on. If you don't, then it is implied that you are being bad, bitter, angry, and so on. If those who did the betraying are not in good recovery, they will often pressure their partner to get over it and forgive them as well. And if she doesn't, the message is that she is now the problem in the relationship.

Forgiving quickly does not speed up or bypass the healing process; it shuts it down. The pain, hurt, and anger do not go away; they just get buried. Emotions are not your enemy. They are there for a reason and need attention. Forgiveness does not get rid of them. You have to feel them to heal them.

Focusing on forgiveness too soon will
shut down your healing process.

It is also important to understand that there is no timeline for healing. The time it takes to heal is different for everyone. If you are early on in the process, give yourself permission to put forgiveness out of your mind for now and focus on your next step in feeling, grieving, and getting support. When it is time, you will feel the desire to forgive naturally rise inside of you. Then, and only then, is it time to lean into forgiveness. And know that forgiveness, ultimately, is about setting yourself free.

I will talk more about forgiveness later, but for right now, stay focused on getting safe, getting help, and getting the truth. That is the first vital step toward healing, and it will let you know what needs to be forgiven at some point. You can't forgive what you don't know.

Trust

Phase One is not the time to focus on trust either. Similar to the incorrect belief that forgiveness will fix everything, there is a misconception many betrayed partners have that if they can just figure out how to trust their partner again, everything will be okay. That is understandable. When betrayal shatters life and your relationship, it is normal to try to grab the pieces and put them back together. According to my HAB survey, 42 percent of betrayed partners had hoped that if they could figure out how to trust him again, things would be okay. Unfortunately, it doesn't work that way.

The thing about trust is that it's different after betrayal. At the start of a relationship, we often *give* trust. We just assume that trust and relationship are one and the same. We give our hearts fully and believe that the other person will honor their end of the deal until life teaches us otherwise.

Trust can be defined as a "psychological state comprising the intention to accept vulnerability based on positive expectations of the intentions or behavior of another."[7] In other words, it is essentially the willingness to be vulnerable with someone because you believe you are safe with them. After betrayal, you no longer have those positive expectations, and it would be dangerous to make yourself vulnerable again this early.

One of the most common questions I get from women who have been betrayed is "Will I ever be able to trust him again?" After betrayal, trust is *earned*, not *given*. It is earned by the consistent trustworthy behavior of your partner over a *long* period of time. The responsibility of rebuilding trust is now on him, not on you. I encourage you to watch his actions because words are cheap, and his promises and intentions are meaningless without action. It's not

7. Denise M. Rousseau et al., "Not So Different After All: A Cross-Discipline View of Trust," *Academy of Management Review* 23, no. 3 (July 1998): 393–404.

what he says but what he does that matters. It is possible for him to rebuild trust, but it is a very long process.

After betrayal, trust is earned, not given.

Like forgiveness, there is often pressure to trust quickly—especially by those who are least trustworthy. He may say, "I'm not doing it anymore. When are you going to trust me again?" This is a type of blame shift, and the reality is these words indicate he is not yet doing true recovery work. He needs to be humble and accept responsibility, not only for his actions but also for how his actions have impacted you. If your partner says anything like this, he is not safe to trust yet. He needs to humble himself, empathize with you, and do the deep character work needed to truly rebuild trust in your relationship. Dr. Peter Kim puts it well in his book *How Trust Works*:

> I don't think repairing trust is always feasible or even the best option. In fact, if someone violates trust, . . . efforts to repair without first addressing the causes and the consequences of what happened can be a recipe for disaster. That would amount to a type of "forced forgetting" in which the harms are likely to persist or recur. . . . That is why, if a violator does not regret the offense, is likely to commit another, and poses a real risk of harm, it can simply make more sense to focus on making oneself less vulnerable to those possibilities by deciding not to trust.[8]

Trusting your partner is not something to push yourself into or focus on in Phase One. At this point of healing, there is a very high likelihood that he is not trustworthy and certainly has not done the

---

8. Peter H. Kim, *How Trust Works: The Science of How Relationships Are Built, Broken, and Repaired* (Flatiron Books, 2023), 193.

work necessary to rebuild trust. Remember that after betrayal, it's not a matter of you deciding to trust your partner again; it's about him acting in a way that proves he's trustworthy over a long period.[9]

Your Partner's Emotions

Phase One is also not the time to focus on your partner's emotions. This is one of the counterintuitive aspects of healing after betrayal that may sound odd, so let me explain. Early on after discovery or disclosure, there is often an unspoken and unconscious balancing act that happens. The question is, whose emotions are going to get center stage? Will the betrayed partner's hurt, confusion, anger, pain, and hopelessness be the focus, or will the betrayer's shame, regret, childhood trauma, or perhaps defensiveness and anger get center stage?

In Phase One, *your* emotions need to be front and center. When this is the case, everyone has a chance to heal. If the focus goes to his emotions, all healing shuts down—his, yours, and the relationship's. This goes against many women's desire to help alleviate their partner's pain. However, when he focuses on your emotions and healing, then he must wrestle with the essential element of empathy: owning what he did *and* what it did to you.

If you focus on his emotions, you lose yourself and healing stops. It is essentially getting out of your shoes and into his shoes. Another way of viewing it is that you would be abandoning your personal circle and jumping into his. Empathy and seeing the world from another person's point of view are beautiful things—but not with your partner right after betrayal. Keep focused on your healing.

Your emotions need to get center stage.

---

9. *Worthy of Her Trust* by Stephen Arterburn and Jason Martinkus is a very good book on this topic. Heads up that it comes from a faith perspective.

It is also crucial for his healing process that he learns to deal with his negative emotions, which he may not have ever learned how to do. That contributes to all forms of intimate betrayal. Shutting down in shame or escalating in anger and defensiveness are ways of avoiding the root issue of his actions and your pain.

There is no healing for the relationship if he is not doing the work. You cannot fix it; you didn't break it. If it is going to heal, he has to do the hard work of getting sober, by which I mean stopping the behaviors that violate your relationship agreement, telling the truth, empathizing with your pain, becoming trustworthy, doing deep character work, learning to work through his own emotions, and healing the damage he has done.

There is absolutely a time and place for him to focus on his emotions. He has to do serious emotional work to heal, and that needs to be done with a qualified professional who has experience helping men heal and grow through sexual integrity issues. What I'm talking about here, however, is where the focus is between the two of you, or as my husband Nathaniel[10] puts it, "who gets the emotional energy."

For example, your partner might say, "I feel so bad that I did all of this to you. I'm a horrible person," as a way of getting you to feel bad for him and make him feel better. In this instance, you can acknowledge his remorse and then let him work through the emotions. That may sound like "Thanks for acknowledging that you've hurt me. I need to go take some time for myself, so I hope you reach out for support to work through what you're feeling."

Your "Stuff"

Phase One is also not the time to focus on your "stuff," meaning the baggage you are carrying from your past. We all have it,

---

10. My husband, Nathaniel Gustafson, did the work to heal and is now a licensed professional counselor and coach who works with men and couples after betrayal (www.TenderheartedMen.com).

though it is different for everyone. It may be a fear of rejection, self-protecting and keeping others at arm's length, or the childhood trauma that left you feeling less than. It also includes all the typical relationship issues of money, sex, communication, and parenting.

You will be tempted to replay every mistake you ever made and every circumstance that could cause guilt or shame. That recurring fight you have about the kids' daycare costs. The chores around the house you kept meaning to do that never got done. The eye rolls you made every time your sister-in-law was around. Were you perfect in your relationship? No. No one is. But now is not the time to focus on that.

If your partner tries to blame you, saying that it is your childhood trauma that is making you respond to the betrayal so strongly, know that he is wrong. Betrayal is a trauma by itself. It may activate memories of past trauma that still need healing, but that does not minimize your current trauma of betrayal, nor should it be held over you. Hold your ground and stay strong. Every other issue is off the table for a time except for the betrayal.

Remember, it is like you are in the hospital on emotional life support. Life pauses. You are fighting to survive and to keep your heart beating. That is more than enough to focus on. Everything else can and needs to wait.

A Reminder for Phase One

As we wrap up Phase One, I want to remind you of one of the foundational truths we started with: *You have great worth and value.* The reality is you are valuable not because of your relationship status, what roles you play, or what you do for others. You have inherent worth and value as a human being.

Intimate betrayal can make you question your worth and value. You were thrown into a battle when betrayal came into your world, and make no mistake—you have to fight. Fight for yourself and for your healing.

Where you land in regard to your belief in your own worth and value is going to significantly impact your healing. But if you do not know where to start from and how to move toward believing in your worth and value, I offer this to you: You can borrow my belief in your worth and value. Sometimes you need others to believe in you until you believe in yourself, so I will hold for you the belief that you have great worth and value until you can hold it for yourself.

Phase Two

Rumble

Sorting Through Broken Pieces

Standing amidst the shattered pieces of your life is over-whelming. Questions flood your mind. *Where do I begin? Is it even possible to heal this?* When the shock subsides, you start sorting through the broken pieces. Which ones will you keep? Which ones will you leave behind? You get to decide. You are creating something new.

Welcome to Phase Two: Rumble. The shift from Phase One to Phase Two happens when you finally have the truth about what your partner has done—or you know that you will never get the truth. Either way, that marks the shift into Phase Two.

You are likely struggling to make sense of everything you've found out, trying to understand how he could have done *this*. You are now digesting this new reality of life as you move into the long, messy middle of Phase Two. Everything is uncertain. You're not sure if you are going to stay or leave, and it's common to wonder if you will ever heal. You may be observing your partner and waiting to see if he is going to do the work to get sober and heal. Emotions are still all over the place, and the grief is still sharp.

This is the Rumble phase.

What you need to hear but may not believe yet is this: It will not always be this intense. You can make it. Hold on and keep going.

In the next three chapters, I'm going to walk you through the keys to navigating Phase Two.

4

Facing the Broken Pieces

A s you move from Phase One to Phase Two—and are trying to absorb the truth of your reality—there can be a unique, even strange, moment of internal silence. Quiet. Numb. A pause amid the pain as your body, mind, and soul try to absorb the information and the reality of what is your life. A movement from one reality to the next.

There is a profound grief that occurs in this transition. There is no longer any doubt that you cannot go back to what was, and yet the future feels intolerable at best, with an unclear timeline or destination.

As you absorb the unimaginable truth and details of your partner's actions, waves of questions may flood your mind as you try to sift through the shattered pieces of your life and heart:

What do I do with all this pain?
How do I move on from here?
Is it even possible to get over this?
Should I stay or should I go?

Is it true that "once a cheater, always a cheater"?

How long will this take?

Can I ever trust him again?

Did he ever really love me?

Was anything real, or was it all a lie?

Why didn't he love me enough to be faithful?

The questions can feel endless and overwhelming. There might also be continuing feelings of shame or self-blame, wondering what you did or didn't do to cause it. This is compounded by society's—and perhaps your partner's—tendency to shift the blame and suggest that you share some responsibility for his acting out.

Hard stop. Remember, this is not your fault. Your partner's betrayal is *never* your fault. Even if he was somehow unhappy, he could have done a thousand things within the relationship to fix it, or he could have asked for a divorce. Instead, he acted out, which is 100 percent on him. When he stepped across the line of your relationship agreement, it was his choice and responsibility—not yours.

In this chapter, I want to come alongside you and help you find your footing. I will help you acknowledge the wait, validate your grief and emotions, deal with triggers, and identify what not to focus on so you can avoid getting stuck. And I want to help you give yourself the tremendous amounts of space, time, and energy required—and that you deserve—to navigate all this and filter through all the questions rumbling in your mind. We will do this together.

Acknowledge the Wait

For those who want to stay in the relationship or who are not sure yet if they want to go, there is an excruciating amount of waiting in the healing process to see if he is going to do the work and become the person you need him to be. Will he stop acting out? Will he take ownership of his actions and the harm he caused you? Will he stop lying and choose to be honest? Will he have empathy and be able to hold space for your pain and anger?

This period of waiting can feel intolerable, particularly if you did not know about the intimate betrayal. It can feel like the man you knew is suddenly gone, and you are now living with a stranger—someone you share everything and nothing with.

For others, his acting out was no secret—or you knew at some level—and you wonder if this nightmare will ever end. After so long, will he finally do the work to get sober and healthy, or is this just part of the pattern of him hurting you over and over again?

Some may be back in this phase because your partner relapsed. The trauma is accumulating, and somehow it feels even more painful. Your hope that this was a one-and-done betrayal has been blown up in yet another relapse. And now you wonder when, if ever, you can trust him again. Now you have to wait for as long as he was sober the last time, and then how much longer beyond that? Maybe now, more than ever, you feel run-down and trapped.

There are any number of scenarios in which you find yourself here at the start of Phase Two. You may be observing and seeing what he will do, but it does not mean you are helpless. There is much you can do for yourself and your healing during this time. Your ability to heal is *not* dependent on whether your partner does his work, nor is it tied to whether the relationship makes it. You can heal.

Validate Your Grief

The grieving process *is* the healing process and is a large focus of Phase Two. The grief of betrayal differs from all other forms of grief though. It's different from losing a sibling or a grandparent. It's different from the grief of a miscarriage. The fact is you may feel that it would have been easier—at least less complicated—if your partner had died. With death, the past and the truth of your relationship remain untouched, while the person left behind has to recalibrate and make sense of a future without their loved one. The grief of betrayal, however, strips you of your past *and* the promise of your future. It wipes out the beautiful moments—or what you thought were beautiful moments. It is grieving the person you thought your partner was. You grieve the sense of safety you once felt. It can feel as if there is no comfort and nowhere to rest. Betrayal entails a grief that is wholly its own.

Grief can be so powerful and intense that it can be difficult to face. It can be tempting to push it aside and not want to deal with it. There may be times when you don't feel strong enough. Grief is interesting in that it is so patient. It simply waits until you are ready to face it. My hope for you, though, is that you choose to do the painful work of grieving now so that you don't have to do it twenty or thirty years from now.

Let me help you unpack the grieving process so you know what to expect.

The grieving process **is** *the healing process.*

Perhaps the most famous understanding of grief comes from psychiatrist Elisabeth Kübler-Ross in her book *On Death and Dying*, first published in 1969. She described grief in terms of five stages. These stages are *not* linear and are *not* meant to be a check-list. You don't move from one to the next in a particular order. Instead, you may find yourself bouncing from stage to stage. The five stages are, in my own words, *shock and denial, anger, bargaining, sadness,* and *acceptance.* Together, they provide a framework for understanding the process of grieving and healing.

Shock and Denial

Shock and denial are the initial shattering we discussed in Phase One when everything that you thought was true—everything you believed about the past—suddenly seems like a lie. This stage is the jolt you feel at discovery or disclosure. There is often a deep sense of numbness and disbelief. You may struggle to straddle two realities: the truth and what you thought was the truth.

Shock and denial are not simply psychological; they are also deeply physical. Shock can appear in the form of shaking, a racing heart, muscle tension, nausea, and more. Denial might be the experience of numbness, a lack of emotion, distracting behaviors, and the like.

Shock and denial are also deeply compassionate ways that your body and mind help you survive by temporarily softening the blow when you are forced to face and absorb the unthinkable. They help to numb the initial blow so that you can fight for what you need in that moment.

Anger

Often, the next stage of grieving is anger, and it is vitally important for healing. It's not only okay to be angry but you will not heal without it. Before we get too far, though, let's get clear on what anger is and what it is not. Anger is not rage. There is a difference. Anger is healthy; rage is not. Anger is necessary for healing; rage is destructive.

By definition, rage is "violent, uncontrolled anger."[1] Many women don't want to feel their anger because they are afraid they will rage and hurt those around them. Perhaps that is you. Or perhaps you have raged and scared yourself and others. If so, there is no judgment, but I recommend that you reach out to a professional who understands betrayal and who can help you connect with your anger in a way that is healthy and promotes healing.

---

1. *Merriam-Webster Dictionary*, "rage," accessed June 13, 2025, https://www.merriam-webster.com/dictionary/rage.

Anger is the most common emotion for betrayed partners to disconnect from. Ironically, anger is the one socially acceptable emotion for men and essentially the one socially unacceptable emotion for women. Many women received negative messages about anger in childhood that impact their ability to connect with their anger and grieve. Three specific themes came out of the HAB survey about these negative messages.

The first theme is that anger is bad or dangerous. Growing up, many learned that anger was harmful, scary, or unacceptable in their family. That often led to fear or avoidance of anger. Examples of this message include

- "Anger isn't going to help."
- "Anger will shame others and not be supportive."
- "Anger is bad."
- "Anger is your problem to deal with alone. Don't speak about being angry."
- "Anger is scary."

The second theme that emerged from the survey was that anger is not acceptable and should be suppressed. Some were hurt physically or emotionally when they expressed their anger. As a result, many learned to deny and bury their emotions. Examples of this message from my HAB survey include

- "My dad was a rager, and my mom showed little emotion at all. I thought emotions were not to be trusted and should be suppressed."
- "We were not allowed to be angry; we got beat."
- "Anger was not allowed in my home growing up. If I felt anger, I had to process it away from anyone else."

The third theme was that anger could only be expressed by some, usually parents or authority figures. Some noted that there was a double standard in their family where parents were allowed to be angry but the kids weren't. Examples of this message include

- "Only my mother could get angry. And my job was to keep her happy, so expressing anger would lead to shame."
- "Anger was a bad emotion and only adults used anger, and it was to punish the children for misbehaving."
- "Anger is a bad thing. My mom demonstrated severe anger toward my dad, which was scary and dangerous at times for me and my siblings."

Even beyond childhood, women are often told or socialized not to be angry but rather to just let things go and move on. In some circles, they are shamed for being assertive and taught to be quiet and submissive. At a fundamental level, this invalidates your emotions and denies that an injustice has occurred. Beyond that, it strips you of your power. This leads many to disconnect with their anger so that it is inaccessible when needed most.

No matter what messages you received about anger, I want to offer this to you: It's okay to be angry. It's *normal* to be angry when your partner betrays you. Not only is it healthy to connect with your anger; it is also necessary for healing.

Many women who never swore before can suddenly find themselves swearing like a sailor, and at times not even the worst profanity seems to do justice to their anger. This is normal. You are not a bad person. As one betrayed partner put it, "The truth is . . . I knew that my anger was my heart's response and attempt to fight off the vileness of betrayal that was attacking my heart. Anger felt so much safer than the intense pain, agony, and helplessness inside me. I was trying to push it out so it didn't kill me. It was me desperately fighting for my heart."

Anger needs to be processed just like any other emotion. The key is to put your thoughts and feelings into words. It may not always come out pretty, but stay connected with your pain, and allow your anger to process and flow through you in healthy ways.

If you shove your anger aside, bury it, or sweep it under the rug, it does not die or go away. It low-grade festers. Buried anger can impact health and healing. It also has the potential to get triggered and shoot up into rage. If it does, then when the rage runs out of steam, it simply goes back underground and the cycle repeats itself. *That* is one way to get stuck in anger. The good news is that at any point, you can get unstuck by putting your thoughts and feelings into words with a safe person.

Just like shock and denial, you don't want to stay in anger forever, but there is a time and place for it. You'll likely return to this stage whenever you're reminded of the terrible injustices that have been done to you. Find healthy support, and allow yourself to feel and work through your anger.

Bargaining

Bargaining is another stage of grief. The stereotypical form of bargaining often sounds like "God, if you will spare my son's life, I'll never do _____ again." Bargaining after betrayal sounds a bit different. It often sounds like conversations you have with yourself in which you attempt to minimize your partner's actions or the pain he caused. For example, *Well, at least his affair was with his coworker and not a prostitute.* Or *At least it was "just" porn.* Or *At least he is a good dad.* It is a way of softening the blow—a way to potentially justify staying in the relationship.

Sadness

This stage of grief is the deep, soul-crushing pain. It is lying in the fetal position on the bathroom floor sadness. Physically, it feels as though you can hardly breathe . . . as if someone is sitting on your chest. You want to hide under the covers and never come out again. Life grinds to a halt, and it feels like the pain will never end. You fear that if you start crying, you'll never stop.

As we discussed in Phase One, sometimes all you can do is just keep breathing. Moment by moment. Breathe in. Breathe out. If you are still surviving moment to moment right now, know that it will not always be this way. It will not always hurt this bad. Keep going. Showers are optional. Do what you need to do to sleep and eat. Feed your kids. Mac and cheese is fine. Keep going.

Your partner's betrayal does not define you.

Acceptance

Acceptance is the stage of grief that everyone wants to get to. It is often associated with "being on the other side." It is the stage of peace and rest from the nightmare you find yourself in. Acceptance is when you no longer try to change, justify, or fight against what you have been through. It is integrating what happened into your story and understanding that the fact of his betrayal is now woven into the fabric of your life. It does not, however, define you.

Everyone reaches acceptance at a different pace. You can't rush this process, but you can get there. You may find that acceptance first comes in little spurts. You may have a moment of peace within yourself, only to be followed with emotions again. You may find yourself fighting against even the idea that this is now part of your story. Again, this is normal. You are still grieving—not just the relationship and your sense of reality and safety as you used to know it but also the story of your own life as you once envisioned it.

You will have moments when denial, shame, anger, bargaining, and sadness resurface—even long after you thought you had resolved those feelings. When that happens, you'll be able to embrace them and allow them to process, returning to the stability of acceptance more easily as time goes on.

Here's the deal about acceptance though: You can't jump ahead or bypass the other stages. This stage is not one you can choose. Instead, it is a by-product of all the work of grieving that you are doing.

Honor Your Emotions

Learning to honor your emotions is an important part of the healing process. Lean in and allow yourself to feel the grief and all the emotions that go with it. The healing process can take a season or a lifetime. It's just a matter of how much you lean in and when you choose to deal with it.

When dealing with the grief, there will be times when you don't feel like you are okay. It's normal to not be okay during this season. There is so much pressure to have it all together. That's not reality though—in life and certainly *not* after betrayal. You don't have to pretend. You don't have to be anything other than who you are. Of course, that doesn't mean you want to be bleeding out to everyone around you, particularly if they are not safe. But give yourself a lot of grace, and when you are able, allow yourself to lean into the emotions rather than run from them or shut them down.

I love the analogy of waves that is often used regarding emotions. When you experience an emotion coming that feels big and scary, picture an ocean wave. As it gets nearer the shore, it grows and looks overwhelming. It looks like it is going to knock you over. Then, right before it hits the shore, the wave crashes, gently sliding up the beach and then gliding back out to sea. Once you've seen the wave a couple of times and know that the emotions will calm, they won't seem quite so scary.

So how do you interact with the wave of those emotions? First, pause. Notice when an emotion comes up and name it. If you are having trouble figuring out what you are feeling, then try this trick:

- Scan your body from head to toe.
- Notice where the tension is in your body.
- Now put a feeling word to that tension (e.g., sadness, anger, fear).

Once you have your emotion, say to yourself or even out loud: *I honor the fact that I feel _____.* You don't need to do anything with it. You don't need to act on it, shame yourself, or push it away. Just hold the emotion with an open hand and get curious about how it feels inside of you. Take a few deep breaths, which will communicate to your brain and body that you are safe. The emotion, like the wave, will eventually subside and dissipate.

Then another emotion might come. Notice it, name it, repeat the process: *I honor the fact that I feel _____.* The act of naming your emotions, sitting with them, and allowing them to come and go *is* the very process of healing.

> *Your emotion, like a wave, will eventually subside and dissipate.*

Pump the Well of Your Soul Dry

Part of healing in Phase Two includes addressing what your mind, body, and soul had to absorb as a result of your partner's acting out. When you discover the truth of what he has done, it is like he takes all of that nasty vileness and deposits it into the well of your soul. If it stays there, it will fester and hurt you. To get it out, you need to "pump the well"[2] of your soul dry. To do that, you need to put your thoughts and feelings into words, preferably with your partner if he is safe.

2. This analogy is from David Clarke, *What to Do When He Says, I Don't Love You Anymore* (Thomas Nelson, 2002), 102–3.

This is not a neat, clean process because what was deposited into your soul was not neat or clean. I never swore at my husband before betrayal. Afterward, I swore like a sailor. They were the only words I could find that expressed my extreme pain and anger, allowing me to get it all out of my body. At times, it felt like even those words weren't strong enough. I'm not sure I could have healed without swearing, but you'll have to decide what feels right for you.

Here's an overlooked truth: *Pumping the well of your soul dry and sharing your thoughts and emotions with your partner is a form of emotional intimacy.* It's not warm and fuzzy, but it is emotional intimacy. Anytime you are sharing your heart with your partner—even the difficult emotions—you are offering him the gift of seeing into your heart. Keep that in mind. Sharing your pain, anger, and sadness is not damaging the relationship—it can be fighting for it.

Safety always comes first though. If it is not emotionally safe to pump the well of your soul to your partner (or if he is abusive or violent), then do not share with him. You do not need to express yourself to him to heal. You do need to express yourself, but it can be in your journal, to a counselor, or with a safe and trusted friend. Your healing is not dependent on your partner. It is helpful if he is present, transparent, emotionally mature, doing the hard work, and generally safe, but you can heal with or without him.

Triggers

Triggers after betrayal can feel absolutely overwhelming. When a trigger hits, it feels like you are back at square one with all the intensity, emotions, and uncertainty. One betrayed partner put it well when she said, "Triggers bring me to my knees. They can paralyze me." The reality is that to find a sense of control in life again, you must deal with triggers.

Triggers are spotlights on areas that still need healing.

My favorite definition of a trigger is something that causes "a strong emotional reaction of fear, shock, anger, or worry in someone, especially because they are made to remember something bad that has happened in the past."[3] Another way to look at it is that triggers are spotlights on areas that still need healing. It's important to note that if your partner acts out or does something new that breaks your trust, that is not a trigger. That is a new breach of trust and an additional wounding.

Many betrayed partners—and the betrayers—feel confused by triggers, which can lead to a sense of shame and frustration. To help mitigate that, let's dive a little deeper into what triggers are and are not.

Triggers are

- a response to wounding
- unpredictable
- spotlights on areas that need healing
- your brain's response to a perceived threat
- a reminder of past hurts

Triggers are *not*

- digging up the past
- holding a grudge
- trying to pick a fight
- being an angry person
- shameful

3. *Cambridge Dictionary*, "trigger," accessed June 8, 2022, https://dictionary.cambridge.org/us/dictionary/english/trigger.

- a sign of lack of forgiveness
- a lack of healing

Consider the analogy of getting a cut or bruise on your arm. Early on, after incurring the wound, if you touch it or if something brushes up against it, it will hurt. Triggers are like that. Triggers are like bumping up against the wound. You will have an instant reaction as you pull back and protect the tender spot. The good news is that, as it heals, it hurts less and less when things bump up against it. Eventually, if something bumps it, you might remember that it used to hurt when that would happen, but it doesn't anymore. As you heal, triggers will gradually become less frequent and less intense and will not last as long. This, however, is largely connected with the degree of safety your partner is proving.

The Brain and Triggers

To understand triggers, it helps to understand a bit about the brain. As we go throughout the day, our brain is constantly taking in information. That information passes through various parts of the brain that interpret, give meaning to, and at times dictate our response to the information. One of the first areas of the brain that information passes through is the amygdala, whose job is to ensure our survival. When the amygdala perceives a threat or danger, it immediately alerts the hypothalamus, which then communicates with the brain stem. The brain stem responds by triggering the release of stress hormones—including cortisol and adrenaline—sending the body into one of several survival responses: fight, flight, freeze, or fawn. As you can see, this is not something you plan, nor is it a decision you make. It happens automatically and immediately at a neurological level as your brain's response to perceived threat.

When your body goes into survival mode, parts of the brain temporarily go offline. This includes the prefrontal cortex, which is the part of the brain that you use to plan and analyze. When the prefrontal cortex goes offline, it impacts your executive functioning, memory, rational thinking, decision-making, and planning. That is why it feels difficult to plan, make decisions, or think through things clearly when you are triggered.

Housed in that part of the brain is the dorsolateral prefrontal cortex with right and left sides. These two areas of the brain are linked to orienting to time. In his book *The Body Keeps the Score*, Van der Kolk explains that "when those areas are deactivated, people lose their sense of time and become trapped in the moment, without a sense of past, present, or future."[4] This contributes to why, when triggered, you feel as if you are back at square one, that it has always been this way, and that it will never change.

When you are triggered, it can feel like you are digressing or losing your mind. You are not. It is trauma. Remember that this is the brain's response to perceived threats, so the key to calming triggers is reestablishing safety—internal and external. Your brain needs to feel that it is safe and that the threat is passed. To do that, you need to calm your brain and your body. The calming practices I shared in chapter 2 can be very helpful for calming triggers.

Triggers for Healing

Triggers feel horrible, and it is normal to just want to make them go away and move past them as quickly as possible. While I completely understand that—and have certainly been in that place—I'd like to offer a thought for you to tuck in the back of your mind. Triggers are there for a reason. As I said earlier, they are spotlights on areas that still need healing. In other words, they tell you the exact issues that are unresolved and that need more focused attention.

I love acting and grew up onstage at my local community theater. During a performance, a spotlight was often used to direct the

4. Van der Kolk, *The Body Keeps the Score*, 69.

audience's full attention to one specific thing or person. Triggers are like that spotlight in that they clearly highlight a specific area to focus on. These are areas that are still wounded. If you notice them and give them compassionate attention, it will help them heal.

In the beginning, triggers come so hard and fast that it is fine to just focus on making it through. But as you continue on and move further along in your healing process, triggers show you your next step of healing. Don't miss these opportunities to gain vital information by pushing through it all as fast as possible.

Another blessing in disguise for those who are further along in their healing process and whose relationship is healing is that triggers can become an invitation for intimacy. If you want to stay in the relationship and your partner has shown that he is emotionally safe, then when you are triggered, you can tell him what is going on and what you need from him. It is an invitation for him to support you.

Triggers can be an invitation for emotional intimacy.

Taking Care of You

We all know that self-care is important, but let's look beyond the clichés here. What does it look like to really take care of yourself, outside of bubble baths and drinking tea (though both can be lovely)? At its core, caring for yourself means doing things that make you feel better. What helps you breathe just a bit deeper? What helps you feel a little calmer? What helps you get back on your feet? There is no right or wrong, and it will look different for everyone. If you are looking for ideas or areas to focus on, though, I have four recommendations: calm your nervous system, focus on your health, find fun again, and embrace your self-worth.

Calm Your Nervous System

Calming your nervous system is key to healing because it helps your brain and body feel safe again. This allows you to come out of fight-or-flight mode and eventually regain a sense of peace and feel present in the moment. There are many ways to calm your nervous system, including deep breathing, mindfulness and meditation, yoga, hiking, and neurofeedback to name a few.

I struggled with this after life blew up. My nervous system felt like it was on fire for about six years. I constantly felt like I was amped up and buzzing, unable to relax and feel calm. I was surviving. I tried several things, but nothing seemed to make a significant difference until I started myofascial release. I was amazed at how calm I felt afterward. Over time, it reset my baseline and allowed my nervous system to remain in a calmer and more rested place. I cannot stress how much I value and appreciate my calm nervous system now.

If you are all too familiar with the feeling of your nervous system being on fire, then you are in good company. But know that it does not have to stay that way, no matter how long it's been. It is possible to feel calm again, but just like I had to try several things until I found what worked for me, you also may need to try different things until you find what works best for you. It is worth the effort.

Focus on Your Health

As I've previously mentioned, betrayal can have a serious impact on your health and well-being. While more research is needed to determine why some end up with medical issues and others don't, you can take major steps to protect yourself by staying on top of doctor appointments. A homework assignment I often give my clients is to write out a list of doctor appointments they need to make, schedule them, and go to them. This may include but is certainly not limited to the following:

- Annual physical
- Pap smear
- Mammogram
- Chiropractic
- Lab work
- Dentist
- Optometrist
- STI test

It is also important to make sure you are eating well, drinking water, and getting enough sleep. When you are in survival mode and working through Phase Two, sometimes the emotional pain is so much that you don't feel like eating or you have trouble sleeping. Or maybe you're overeating and oversleeping. Wherever you are, I invite you to give yourself grace and take even just one step to shift toward taking care of your body and physical health.

Find Fun Again

One aspect of life often lost with betrayal is the ability to have fun. Betrayal often steals fun and shuts off playfulness. In my HAB survey, 98 percent of betrayed partners reported that betrayal *negatively impacted* their ability to have fun. And 32 percent said it *completely impacted* their ability to have fun. Even after the crisis is over, many betrayed partners' baselines remain in a heavy place, so much so that they don't even recognize they are missing out on fun and playfulness.

The loss of playfulness and fun happens on a neurological level, as the shock of betrayal throws the nervous system into fight-or-flight mode. The nervous system can get stuck in an activated state even after the danger is gone. Purposely reengaging in fun helps move the brain into a more flexible and resilient space.

I rediscovered fun after betrayal through indoor skydiving. My husband took me for my birthday several years into the healing process. I remember standing at the entrance of the wind tunnel, raising my arms in the air, and leaning into the wind. The instructor stabilized me as I flew with my arms outstretched, and the solid pressure of the wind on my body held me in the air several feet off the ground. It was incredible. I couldn't stop smiling and was instantly hooked. When I got out of the tunnel it felt like every cell in my body had come alive. I remember telling Nathaniel, "Oh my gosh, this is what fun feels like! I forgot. I forgot what it felt like to have fun!" Flying gave me my spark back, and I have been flying ever since. I am forever grateful for the outlet to embrace fun and playfulness again.

About a year ago, I decided to introduce a friend to flying as well. She had recently learned of her husband's betrayal and was understandably struggling. I flew out to meet her and we hung out and talked. But since I believe that fun is crucial to healing, we also went indoor skydiving. We laughed as the instructor handed us the one-size-fits-none jumpsuits, and then I watched as she stood at the entrance of the tunnel, raised her arms, and leaned into the wind. Her face instantly lit up with a familiar smile. I watched as she giggled and floated in the wind. For a moment, it was as if all the pain and darkness she was facing had faded away. Afterward, she hugged me and thanked me for taking her flying. "It gave me hope," she said. "If I can smile and giggle amid everything that's happening, maybe I'll be okay." The fun didn't change the situation or take her pain away, but it helped her rise out of it for a moment and gave her hope that there is life on the other side.

What is fun for you? What used to bring you joy? What makes you laugh and smile? Feel free to explore and try something new that could help you tap into playfulness and fun again. I know it may feel like the last thing you need to focus on right now, but I invite you to give yourself permission to find fun again and experience that glimmer of hope.

Reclaiming fun is a key aspect of healing.

Embrace Your Self-Worth

Betrayal deals a devastating and intimate blow to your self-worth, so we must face this issue head-on. You may be thinking, *That sounds great, but I have no idea how to do that.* If you are having a hard time connecting with your sense of worth, here are two counterintuitive questions to get you pointed in the right direction:

First, are you disconnected from your anger?

Anger and self-worth often go hand in hand, so if you are disconnected from your anger, you are likely disconnected from your self-worth. Anger tells you that something is wrong, and it fuels a righteous indignation that says, "Wait a second, that's not okay. I don't deserve to be treated this way." When you connect with your anger, you can start to connect with your self-worth.

Second, are you giving your worth and value to others?

When you feel stuck, it's possible that you are giving your worth to others in the sense that in order for you to be okay and feel good about yourself, others have to think about you and respond to you in a certain way. By doing so, you lose your power.

I want to take this out of the betrayal world for a moment and share how this played out with Melissa.[5] She and a group of friends were hanging out at a park watching their kids run around the playground, yelling happily. She shared about their recent vacation to Cabo, and one of the other moms made a comment under her breath about how it must be nice to have enough money to go on vacations like that. Melissa pretended that she didn't hear it, but she was hurt and offended. She pulled back and was quiet for the rest

---

5. The person's name and identifying details have been changed or presented in composite form to ensure privacy, safety, and anonymity.

of the time. She realized, though, that since they were friends and she valued their friendship, she needed to say something.

Later that day, she called her friend and told her that her comment had hurt her and she would like to talk about it. The conversation didn't go well. The other mom got defensive and went on the attack, saying Melissa was being too sensitive and putting words in her mouth. Melissa left the conversation even more upset and kept replaying it in her mind, wishing she could go back and set her straight.

Together, we debriefed the situation and the way that Melissa was giving her friend the power to determine whether she was okay. I had Melissa visualize reaching out and taking her self-worth from her friend and putting it back in her personal circle. She then had the power to look at what was going on and how she could nurture that part of her. She was slowly able to take responsibility for her emotional well-being and allow her friend to have her own emotions even if she didn't agree with them. She could choose to be okay no matter how her friend felt about the situation.

In regard to betrayal, we often give our partner, friends, or family our worth and value. We think we cannot feel okay about ourselves unless they feel okay with us. We need to separate that feeling out. We must decide that we do have worth and value, whether or not our partner, friends, or family believe it.

As you lean into your worth and value, here are a few things to remember. I encourage you to write them down and say them out loud to yourself:

- I *am* enough.
- I *am* worthy of love.
- I *am* worthy of happiness.
- I *am* worthy of faithfulness.

- I *am* worthy of being fought for.
- I have *great* worth and value.

What Not to Focus On

Phase Two is long and overwhelming at times. Just as with the previous phase, there are certain things that are important to focus on, but there are also things *not* to focus on. My goal is to keep you moving through the healing process as quickly and smoothly as possible, so let's shift our focus to four things that can slow down or stall out your healing process in Phase Two.

Being Okay

In Phase Two, your relationship is not okay, you are not okay, and it's okay that you are not okay. Be very gentle with yourself. There is so much pressure on women to act like everything is fine and they have everything under control. The reality is betrayal is brutal. You're in the thick of it in Phase Two, and you may not know what is going to happen with your relationship yet. So in case you need permission, it's okay to pull back and make life smaller for a while. It is okay if you are not up for hanging out with friends or you can't perform at work like you normally do. Give yourself permission to not be okay for a season, to take care of yourself, and to focus on healing.

The Decision to Stay or Go

It is important to think about whether you want to stay in the relationship after betrayal. If you're like most, you never dreamed your partner would betray you and that you'd feel like you don't know who he is anymore. As you sort through everything and consider whether this is a relationship you want to continue in, all options are on the table.

Considering if you want to go or stay in the relationship after betrayal is not bad—it's a necessity. Where it can become a stuck point is if it becomes all you can think about and it distracts from the rest of your healing. Of course, you can decide at any time, but if you feel like you are stuck and spiraling on this decision, it may be helpful to table it for a certain period of time. Maybe that is a month, three months, or six months. You get to decide the time frame that feels right to you. It also does not mean that you need to make a decision at the end of this period of time, but you can revisit the question then. In the meantime, it frees you to lean into the grief and focus on your healing without feeling the constant pressure of making a decision.

Your Partner's Recovery Actions

Ironically, this is not the time to focus on his recovery actions. This one may sound odd, so let me explain. He needs to be working hard, but what you need from him is not checking the box of recovery work but true heart change. Many women, particularly as they get further into Phase Two, feel confused when they see their partner doing recovery actions, such as going to counseling, attending group meetings, or listening to podcasts, but still responding in angry and defensive ways and not empathizing with her emotions.

These women often hear from their partners, "I'm doing everything you've asked me to do. What more do you want?" or "Nothing I do will ever be good enough for you." It is not the number of recovery activities he is doing that is key but whether those activities are resulting in heart and character changes.

Sobriety is not the finish line—it is the starting line. He doesn't get kudos for no longer breaking your relationship agreement. He never should have done that in the first place. Healing requires so much more. If there is going to be any safety or healing in the relationship, then he has to do the deep character work. That includes understanding the root cause and his personal "why" that motivated his acts of betrayal, which usually tie back to childhood. Safety and healing in your relationship also means he must do the hard work of learning to be humble, taking ownership, offering kindness and empathy to you, and being able to sit with you in your emotions without defensiveness. That is what character work looks like.

Sobriety is not the finish line—it is the starting line.

Your Partner's Emotions

It is still not the time to focus on your partner's emotions. This is similar to Phase One but with a few twists. Instead of the pull being to focus on his feelings of shame and regret, in Phase Two there is often pressure for you to stop acting or responding in a certain way so that he does not have to face your pain. There are a few different ways this might sound.

Your reaction is hurting me.

When you get in touch with your emotions and start to express them, it is not uncommon for your partner to push back. He may take a victim stance and say that your expression is hurting him. This is a form of blame shifting. They put the focus on your anger or sadness and imply you are being mean, which takes the focus off the fact that their actions were the source of your pain and anger.

This is often perpetuated by therapists who focus on the relationship rather than the betrayal. If they don't understand betrayal, then a well-meaning therapist can focus on your anger being the problem rather than holding him accountable for his actions and focusing on his betrayal.

At the core of intimate betrayal is his lack of willingness to deal with negative emotions. To heal, he must learn to face that and grow through it. By expressing your emotions, you are allowing him to work on it in real time. His reaction to your emotions is for him to work through with a qualified professional. It's not your job to manage his emotions or prevent him from feeling difficult things.

I need to focus on my childhood trauma, not your pain.

As men start to focus on themselves and how they got to where they are, childhood trauma often surfaces. This does not mean that all men who act out sexually were abused or molested as children. That is not true. However, when varying degrees of childhood trauma are identified, the focus can shift from healing the betrayal to healing his trauma. When that happens, it can become a trump card, or he can lose sight of your pain and the need to heal the damage he has done to the relationship. Betrayed partners often feel that they must put their needs and desires aside once again and allow all the focus to go to his healing.

The reality is that while it's very important for him to address his childhood trauma, he does not get to abandon you and your pain in the process. Nor should the betrayal healing be put on pause while he does it. At best, that is a lack of balance. At worst, it is a convenient way for him to avoid the pain and damage he has caused you. He likely spent decades ignoring the childhood trauma, so now is not the time for it to take center stage. If he wants to heal the relationship, then he cannot leave you alone in your pain. He can seek guidance from his counselor or support system on how he can do his personal work and not abandon you in the process.

I See You

As we wrap up this chapter, I want to just say that I see you. I see your pain and the work you have to do to heal from what your partner did to you. I hear the deep weariness of having to grieve one more thing. I recognize the loss of innocence—or at the very least peace—as you are thrown into a world you may never have known existed. I see you as you try to hold it together while playing with your kids or leading the meeting at work. I acknowledge the deep injustice of it all. So take a moment and rest. Go hide under the covers and let yourself cry. Then take a deep breath, dig deep, stand up straight, and go fight for yourself. One day—one moment—at a time. I see you. You've got this.

5

His Work

After life blew up, my husband and I were fortunate to get really good help quickly. We saw our counselor twice a week for months, and some weeks, even that didn't feel often enough. The question I asked our counselor the most was "What is going on with him? You've got to help me understand."

That was not me trying to stay in my head and deny my emotions or intellectualize the experience. If I was going to stay in the seemingly black hole of searing pain long enough to see if he was going to change, I needed someone to shine a light on this new, foreign, treacherous path I was transported to against my will. Thankfully, our counselor skillfully interpreted what I was seeing and experiencing with my husband, and it helped calm me during those moments.

We'll turn to your partner in this chapter, but this is not to shift the focus to him. In this phase, your focus needs to stay on you. The reality is, though, you are likely still interacting with your partner, and what he does or does not do has a significant impact on you. I want to help you understand what is going on with him to help ground you in the storm and to help you know what to look for.

First, a word of caution: Understanding does not take the pain away. You cannot heal your heart with your head. Facing the pain and grieving it is the only way to calm it. However, this path of healing often feels completely disorienting, so I am going to pass on some insights that will help clear up some of the chaos and confusion and get your feet back underneath you.

You cannot heal your heart with your head.

Understanding Intimate Betrayal

Let's go back to the first foundation that I outlined in the introduction to the book: Your partner's betrayal is not your fault. Ever. To help you understand more about why that is true, let's unpack some background about the nature of intimate betrayal and sexual acting out. Before I do that, though, let's be clear that understanding it does not excuse it. Even if bad things happened to him as a child, at some point it became his responsibility to heal those wounds. His decisions are fully on him.

Intimate betrayal and sexual acting out is not about sex or beautiful women. It is deeper than that. It is about your partner's pattern of not dealing with wounds and negative emotions, usually rooted in childhood. What happens for some men is that as children, life was overwhelming, and they did not know how to handle it or didn't have the support they needed. At some point, they discovered that porn, sex, or objectifying women could make all the feelings of rejection, loneliness, boredom, sadness, and anger go away—for a moment. As that pattern of using sexual arousal to soothe negative emotions was repeated, it eventually became ingrained. Over time, a link was formed in their brain's neural pathways between

116

the difficult emotions and their subsequent behaviors, leading to numbing out and escaping through sexual activity as a way of dealing with and soothing those emotions. As they continued, the link became a highway in the brain—a familiar, well-worn path.

Your partner's betrayal has nothing to do with you, as the pattern was probably in place long before you even met him. The pattern of acting out and the neural pathways in his brain were already in motion. His acting out would have happened no matter who he was with. And to stop it requires a massive shift beyond just deciding he won't do it anymore.

I want to pause and acknowledge, though, that nothing feels more personal than intimate betrayal. And it is still not your fault. You did not cause it. It had nothing to do with your body or not being enough as a partner or sexual being. The inevitable ways you were not perfect in the relationship—because no one is—did not cause him to betray you. The patterns for his actions were set long ago. He broke your relationship agreement, and he bears the responsibility for his actions and the damage he caused you.

Myths

There are many myths around intimate betrayal and how to "fix it." I hope that naming and debunking some of these myths will bring you further clarity.

Myth #1: Getting married will fix his sexual integrity issues.

Truth: Getting married does not heal or change his dysfunctional relationship with sex. If he had sexual integrity issues before getting married, he will bring them into the relationship and continue them. There might be a period of time that he does not engage in them, but unless he has done the deep work of healing, he will act out again.

Myth #2: We can fix this together.

Truth: You cannot fix or heal this in him. Only he, with the help of a specialized therapist or coach, can address his core issues and change his behavior. Without that, true sobriety will not happen because the root causes of his behavior remain. His sobriety alone is insufficient, and your focusing on his healing will halt your own progress.

Myth #3: If he is really sorry and remorseful, he won't do it again.

Truth: Feeling sorry for what he has done and stopping his behavior are two different things. It is important for your partner to say he is sorry, but those are just words. He has to take action to change. Saying "I'm sorry, I won't do it again" is never enough and cannot be trusted without consistent action to back it up.

Myth #4: I just need to figure out how to trust him and put this behind me, and we'll be fine.

Truth: Choosing to trust your partner and put his betrayal behind you does not heal it. In fact, it almost guarantees that neither of you will heal. The only way for him to fully heal and provide safety in the relationship is for him to do the deep, hard work of healing. That includes owning his actions and the impact they had on you, understanding his "why," changing his thoughts and behaviors, and doing the deep character work of empathy and humility, to name a few. Furthermore, after betrayal, trust needs to be earned over a long period of time.

Myth #5: He just needs to pray or meditate more.

Truth: This is called spiritual bypassing. Many men in faith communities have been told that if they just read the Bible, pray, and meditate more, they will no longer struggle. Then when it doesn't work, they feel an even deeper level of shame, isolation, and powerlessness. There is a path to healing, but it almost always requires specialized help and deep work over a significant period of time.

What Good Recovery Looks Like

It is very helpful to know what good recovery looks like in your partner so you can determine if he is actually healing. This is crucial, as it has a deep impact on your life and your decisions moving forward.

Sobriety

First, he needs to get sober. Sober means that he has stopped acting out of any and all behaviors that violate your relationship agreement.

Remember, sobriety is not the finish line—it is the starting line. There is no healing without safety, and there is no safety without sobriety. Sobriety doesn't provide safety though; it simply gives the opportunity for safety to develop if he continues to do the deeper work of healing.

Second, he needs to stay sober. As long as he continues to act out or relapse, the damage will continue. Trauma is cumulative, and the compounding damage that relapses do to a betrayed partner is devastating.

The pain of betrayal is so intense. No one wants to go through it even once, let alone repeatedly. According to the HAB survey, 22.4 percent said their partner had not relapsed. Another 22.3 percent said they did not know. Of the 55.3 percent who responded that their partner had relapsed, 19.8 percent said it happened 1–3 times, 7.9 percent said 4–6 times, 3.1 percent said 7–9 times, and 24.5 percent said 10 or more times.

How many times, if at all, has your (ex-)partner relapsed since you found out about the betrayal?

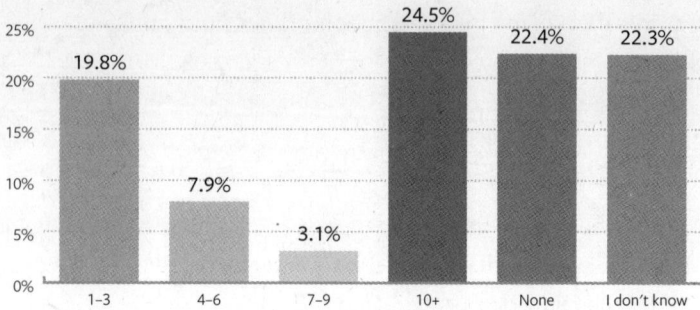

It is possible for men to get sober and stay sober. Many betrayed partners are told they should not set the bar too high. Many are given the expectation that they need to accept when he relapses and continue in the relationship as long as he says he's sorry, gets back on the wagon, and so on. In fact, in that same survey, 57 percent of betrayed partners were told by a helping professional or faith leader that "relapse is a part of recovery." Of those who received that message, 60 percent said it was harmful, and 24 percent said it was helpful.

For those who found the message harmful, the themes that emerged were that they were frustrated because it made excuses for their partner's harmful behavior, that their pain was minimized, and that the destructive patterns of how they were treated were overlooked. As a result, many lost faith in counseling and helping professionals and were left with overwhelming feelings of powerlessness and the desire for their partner to be held accountable for his actions.

Here is what some partners said who found it harmful:

- "For us, hearing that relapse was part of recovery, my husband took the view he could occasionally just not deal with his emotions and instead act out. He didn't have to always be truthful or forthcoming with me. It was like someone said me continuing to be hurt was just part of the process, as if that is acceptable."

- "It makes me feel like, what is the point in trying to make our marriage work then? I don't want to go through this pain again."
- "After twenty-five years of repeated betrayal, it made me feel like I was expected to just keep sucking it up, even though I never saw any real work toward change or felt any remorse or empathy."
- "It seemed to give him permission and to coerce me into denial of the devastation of repeated betrayal."

For those who found the message helpful, the themes that emerged from the survey were an appreciation of the concept of recovery being a journey rather than a one-time achievement, that it helped them separate their partner's actions from their self-worth, and that it helped them understand their partner's behaviors. However, even among those who found it helpful, there was also the acknowledgment that it was very difficult emotionally, and it created additional fear and mistrust.

Here is what some partners said who found it helpful:

- "In many respects, it makes sense to me because I understand that you don't always get something to stick the first time."
- "It helps me to understand the nature of addiction and to detach from it being about me. It is not anything I do or do not do that causes relapse."
- "Initially, it was harmful. I was terrified. But it was the truth. It has since set me up for the reality of this disease and what it means to be married to an addict."
- "It was helpful and harmful. Helpful because it let me understand it was a normal part of healing. Harmful as it kept me fearful, suspicious, and less trusting."

The fact is you get to decide what is acceptable in your relationship and what your heart can handle. No one—not your partner, a helping professional, a faith leader, or a family member—gets to tell you what you need to accept or not accept in your relationship. You are the only one living your life. You get to make whatever decisions are right for you.

> *You get to decide what is acceptable in your relationship and what your heart can handle.*

Character Change

Let's assume for a moment that he is no longer acting out. What now? What does it mean for him to do the work of recovery beyond sobriety? It is the deeper heart and character change. It is a change you can feel even if you can't put it into words. You don't simply need action; you need his heart to undergo transformation if he is going to be worthy of your heart.

The first aspect of good recovery work (aka character change) is seen in how he treats you. It is him having humility, patience, and kindness toward you and your healing process. He no longer attacks or blames you but fully owns not only what he has done but also the impact it has had on you. It is him doing his own emotional work so he can have empathy for you and learn how to sit with you in your pain and anger without getting defensive. There is no longer pressure to hurry up and heal, to stop talking about it, to forgive and trust, or to have sex with him.

A second aspect of the work of character change is him digging deep to understand why he did it and what he needs to do so that it doesn't happen again. It is knowing and anticipating his triggers and having a solid plan in place to deal with them in the future. It is learning the root of the issue, which almost always starts in childhood and has deep ties to family of origin issues. This is part of him knowing his "why," and it is so important. There is no safety if he does not know his core wounds, how they impact him, and what to do about them.

A third aspect of good recovery work includes him doing inner child work so he can help the little boy inside of him to grow up. This may seem odd and unnecessary for men who are new to this process, but I assure you that this is a vital step. Sexual acting out stunts emotional development, and a part of them stays at that development level. If this is unclear, think back to the last time he acted out or when you two had a fight. How old did he feel to you? Have you ever felt like he was treating you as if you were his mom? Almost without fail, men who have sexual integrity issues have a part of them they need to help grow up. And until they do, their sobriety—and your heart—will always be in danger.

Unfortunately, the deeper character change does not happen overnight. The core character work requires laying down a new foundation of health: demolishing the old and extensively excavating all that has been buried, all the skeletons he has been hiding and running from. Here's the deal though: If he is doing the work, it will be obvious.

Across the street from my office a storage facility was torn down so apartments could be built in its place. It has been a very loud, intrusive, observable two-year process. There was no mistaking the fact that work was happening. First, they brought in huge tractors to demolish the storage units. The sound of the walls caving in, then being scraped up and dumped into one of a huge line of trucks to be hauled away was unmistakable. The next round of scraping up the debris and digging up the old foundation was intrusive as they closed the road for a new round of construction vehicles. Finally, they installed a massive thirty-story crane to haul the construction materials up to the new levels they were building. Pallets of construction materials slowly swinging past my window during sessions were a constant reminder of what was happening.

A final product takes time to build, but the fact that work is being done and is headed in a particular direction is wildly obvious for the apartment building outside my office window—and the same is true for men in good recovery. You will see and feel the effects of good recovery without having to squint hard or wonder if it is happening. It may be messy and slow at times, but you can see and feel it. If you do have to look hard, then that is an indication he is not digging deep enough or working hard enough and therefore is not in good recovery.

> *You will see and feel the effects of good recovery without having to squint hard or wonder if it is happening.*

Dealing with Shame

Many men struggle with feeling shame about acting out, and sometimes the shame itself becomes a block in healing. If he goes into a shame spiral about what a horrible person he is, it can lead to self-pity and pull the emotional focus back on himself. Both shut down the healing process. His feelings of shame may be very real, but he needs to face his shame and work through it with the help of a qualified counselor. This is crucial for his long-term health and recovery. He also cannot be present with your emotions if he is consumed by his shame.

Your partner should not look to you for help dealing with his shame. You are not in charge of taking care of his heart—and certainly not his sobriety. He needs to have a group of healthy, solid men in place with whom he can be vulnerable and get support. This is not a typical "accountability group" in which no one is really sober and the main topic of conversation is how their partners are being mean to them. That is not safe or healthy. What I'm talking about is a group—usually facilitated by a therapist—that can ask him the hard questions and point him toward integrity. If he does not have a group of men like that now, then I highly recommend that he find one. There are many groups out there, and this step is vital for your safety and his recovery.

When He's NOT in Good Recovery

The easy answer to what it looks like when a man is *not* in good recovery is the opposite of what good recovery looks like. For the sake of clarity, though, here are some things that would indicate he is not doing the work. This is not a complete list, of course, but it will give you an idea of some key yellow and red flags to be looking for.

- Continuing to break your relationship agreement
- Not taking ownership of what he did
- Not taking ownership for what it did to you
- Blaming you for his actions in overt or subtle ways (e.g., "It was after the baby was born, and you weren't having sex with me.")
- Continued gaslighting
- Refusal to give a full disclosure or take a polygraph
- Anger or intimidation toward you or others
- Pressure to have sex with him
- Lack of humility or kindness
- Pulling away from you
- Continued secrets or lack of transparency
- Scaring or hurting you[1]

---

1. If he is hurting, controlling, or scaring you, that is abuse. I recommend reaching out to a professional, because men who are abusive often become more abusive when they are confronted. Seek immediate help if you or your children are ever in danger. If you are in the United States, call 911. You can also call the National Domestic Violence Hotline at 800-799-7233 or text BEGIN to 88788.

- Putting demands or expectations on you (e.g., you need to forgive, address your childhood trauma, speed up your healing process, etc.)

Trust Your Gut

I encourage you to trust your gut. It is the best indication of whether he is doing good work. The reality is you don't need another book, podcast, counselor, or coach, your mom, or certainly your partner to tell you if he is changing. You will feel it. Sometimes, listening to everyone else makes things more confusing. You are the one who knows best, and it is something that you feel at a deep, heart level. You know if he is being kind or if he is putting the blame on you. You know when he feels sincere or when it feels like he is just repeating the words the counselor told him to say. You know if he feels the same or if you go, *Huh. That's different.*

Perhaps you are reading this and thinking, *No. I don't know. I thought he was doing good work before and then he acted out, so I can't tell.* If you resonate with that, it makes complete sense that you struggle to trust your gut. I encourage you not to give up though. Learning to listen and respond to your gut is a crucial part of your healing, so if this feels scary or unattainable, I encourage you to reach out to a professional who specializes in this area so they can help you navigate this.

Why Can't You Get Over It?

Here is one thing that still blows my mind: Men who are not in good recovery all say and do the same things. It doesn't matter what country they are from, how old they are, or their socioeconomic status. It is like they are all reading from the same book. The good news is that these patterns make it very easy for a professional who specializes in this area to quickly assess where he is at in his healing process.

One of the most common pressures you will get from a man who is not in good recovery is to put himself in the victim role and to pressure you to get over what he has done without him doing the real work of healing. It will likely come out in some version of the following:

- "I'm not doing that anymore. Why can't you get over it?"
- "I'm a changed man (implying that you should stop _____)."
- "Why can't you move on?"
- "Let's put that in the past."
- "It's been long enough. You should be further along."
- "Your anger is abusive to me."
- "My therapist said I need to set boundaries with you."

This type of pressure comes from a man who does not want to take full responsibility or ownership for the impact of his actions or do the deep, necessary work to heal. It is also a subtle (or not so subtle) form of gaslighting, making you feel you are the problem. If your partner is pressuring you to move on or making you feel guilty about your healing, then that is a serious sign he is not doing the character work needed. If he truly wants to heal the relationship, he will need the help of a qualified professional who also understands what betrayed partners go through.

Abuse

Abuse is the ultimate example of a betrayer who is not in good recovery. Abuse has long been overlooked in the world of betrayal healing. Unfortunately, that has left many betrayed partners alone in very difficult and at times dangerous situations.

In my research survey of 1,729 betrayed partners, 87 percent said they experienced some form of abuse in their relationship. More specifically, 20 percent reported physical abuse, 34 percent reported sexual abuse, 68 percent reported emotional abuse, and 88 percent reported psychological abuse. A total of 11 percent reported they had experienced all forms of abuse listed. Similar results were found in a study of betrayed partners by Lisa Taylor and Irene De Haan published in 2023.[2] If you can relate to those results and have experienced—or are currently experiencing—abuse, there are a few things I want you to know:

- No one has a right to treat you that way. It is not okay for him to hurt you.
- You matter. Your safety matters.
- You are not alone. Unfortunately, this is not uncommon, which means that there are others who understand and can help.
- His abuse is not your fault. He may go to great lengths to tell you that it is and to blame it on you, but his abuse is never your fault.

As I've mentioned before, if you are experiencing this, I highly recommend that you shift your focus to your safety and the safety of your kids (if you have them and they are still at home). Reach out to your local domestic violence shelter or a therapist who specializes in abuse to get the help and guidance you need.

Pause and Hope

Before we move on, I want to offer hope and answer a question I get a lot from betrayed partners: "Is it possible for men to change

2. Lisa Taylor and Irene De Haan, "The Prevalence of Domestic Violence in the Lives of Female Heterosexual Partners of Sex Addicts," *Violence Against Women* 29, nos. 15–16 (September 2023). In this study, 92.1 percent reported that they had experienced some form of domestic violence at the hands of the person who betrayed them. In addition, 57.7 percent reported having experienced physical and/or sexual intimate partner violence in their relationship.

and heal?" Yes, it is possible. I have seen incredible transformation in men when they dig in and do the work. That includes men who are older or have been acting out for decades. Healing and change are possible. Not all men, however, will choose to do the work. It is very important to take his actions at face value. It is not his potential that is important—it is his actions. But is it possible if he decides to do the work to heal? Yes.

6

Your Healing

A fundamental part of healing after betrayal is stepping into your power. My desire is to help you step into that power, which will greatly impact your life whether or not you decide to stay in the relationship.

Intimate betrayal, at its core, involves an imbalance of power. Power is the ability to influence or to resist influence. When your partner betrayed you, he held the power, even if you didn't know it. His deeds became the most prominent and influential actions in your relationship, with painful and far-reaching effects. For those who hid their betrayal, they held the power by blocking your ability to influence them. Some betrayed partners know about their partner's acting out, but despite their pleas or demands, their partner continues to act out or relapse. This is also resisting influence.

My desire for you is that you have control over your life—yourself—and have the ability to design a future you are excited to live in.

Finding Your Voice

Betrayal shatters the good. We know that. But the reality is that it shatters the bad as well. It shatters the old, well-worn, and unhelpful patterns of being and relating. This allows room for new patterns to be established. No more staying silent. No more playing small. It is the time to find your voice.

Betrayal shatters the good, but it also shatters the bad.

At the core, finding your voice is putting your thoughts and feelings into words. Whether you grew up shy, your voice was silenced as a child, or betrayal took your breath away, the message that many women get is that they should be small and quiet. No more. What you want and need matters. Your safety matters. Your desires matter. And part of your healing is to put all of that into words.

Sometimes the hardest part is mentally, emotionally, and physically willing the words to come out of your mouth. If you are used to being silent, start by just opening your mouth and getting used to expressing yourself. One of my favorite quotes, often attributed to American activist Maggie Kuhn, is "Speak your truth, even if your voice shakes." Don't be ashamed if your voice shakes. Instead, I encourage you to view it as a success that you dared to speak.

There may come a point in the journey of finding your voice when you will experience a pendulum swing and feel that you came across too strong. That's okay. It is a sign of progress and finding your way. Sometimes you may overshoot and come across as too strong, while other times you might undershoot and feel you didn't stand up for yourself and speak as strongly as you wanted to. Each time you find your voice, you will learn. Course correct and keep going. It will become smoother the more you do it. You get to give yourself the gift of finding your voice and figuring out how to use it most effectively.

Trusting Your Gut

I mentioned trusting your gut in the previous chapter, but let's dive in a little deeper. Most betrayed women have experienced a lot of gaslighting, which makes you question your reality. This can lead to not trusting yourself or your gut, which further robs you of your power. Learning to trust your gut is a crucial part of healing—not only of healing from betrayal but also of healing your relationship with yourself.

Trusting your gut means listening to your intuition. It means that when something feels off, you pay attention to it. It means that you are the author of your reality. No one else gets to tell you what is true or that you are overreacting or crazy or making something up. Your gut is that quiet voice inside of you or that queasy feeling in your stomach.

As you start down the path of reconnecting with your gut, think back on times when you felt something was off and later found out you were right. Choose to see that as a win now. Your gut was right. Be gentle with yourself. It doesn't matter if you dismissed it then; you are listening to it and learning from it now. This is a big step toward trusting yourself again.

Next time your gut is telling you that something is off, pause and get curious. Notice if you hear the echo of someone's voice telling you to ignore it. Choose instead to trust yourself or at least hold space that your gut could be right. Then notice how it plays out. Each time you see that your gut is right, it will help strengthen your trust and belief in yourself. And if there are times that your gut is not 100 percent accurate, learn from that, but do not give up. Your gut is critically important.

Trust your gut.

Forgiveness

In Phase One, I said not to focus on forgiveness, that if you focused on it too early, it would stall your healing process. Things start to shift in Phase Two in this regard. Once you have the full truth—or the knowledge that your partner refuses to give you the full truth—and are acknowledging your anger and working through your grief, then when you are ready, your focus can safely shift to forgiveness. Please hear me, though, that it is still important that you do not rush the process or move forward based on pressure or guilt messages from your partner or anyone else.

There are many myths and misunderstandings about forgiveness, so let's start by getting a clear understanding of what it is and what it is not.

What Forgiveness Is Not

It does not mean "forgive and forget."

Unfortunately, many betrayed partners—particularly in faith communities—are told that they need to forgive and forget. That doesn't work. It's not possible. We cannot delete memories from our minds. It is also not safe. It is essentially saying to deny your emotions and move forward as if nothing happened. It also gives the message that you should not make future decisions based on past experiences. That is risky at best and dangerous at worst. It also lets your partner off the hook without dealing with the consequences of his actions.

It will not stop the pain.

Forgiveness does not stop the pain. The only way through the pain is through it. Forgiveness is, at times, an actionable part of the healing process—a vital step in freeing ourselves from the shackles of unresolved pain. But it is also an organic outcome of the healing work you've done; it's a point of time you naturally come to in the process of doing the hard work of healing your heart. But one thing that forgiveness is not: It is *not* a way out of the pain.

It is not the way to heal the relationship.

Many betrayed partners are told—or perhaps believe themselves —that if they could just forgive their partner for what he did, then the relationship would be healed and they would be able to move forward almost as if it didn't happen. Forgiveness does not heal the relationship. If the relationship is going to heal, then he needs to put in the work to heal it.

It does not equal reconciliation.

The idea that forgiveness equals reconciliation is one of the most widespread and powerful misconceptions about forgiveness. Some people are not safe or healthy and should not be in your life. You do not have to continue to give someone access to your life, your heart, or your mind when they have proven to be unsafe. You get to choose how you want to proceed. You can forgive them and not talk to them again. Or you can forgive them and continue in your relationship with them, redefining your boundaries and never again letting them into the sacred inner space of your heart. Or you can forgive them and over time—and with a lot of work on their part—allow them full access back into your heart. All scenarios, and everything in between, are possible. You get to decide what is right for you.

It does not mean you won't feel sad or angry anymore.

Forgiveness is not a tool to shut off your emotions. You will have emotions—even difficult ones—after you forgive. It does not mean that you have not forgiven. It means that there is more to grieve.

Get curious about what is coming up inside of you and see what needs healing and attention.

It does not mean you will never bring it up again.

If the relationship is going to heal and be healthy in the long term, you must have the freedom to bring up the betrayal and talk about it any time for as long as you need to. This does not mean you are beating a dead horse for the rest of your life. It is about the freedom to fully heal. Months or even years later, there will be things that remind you of the past or questions may come up. It needs to be open for discussion at any time. The ability to bring up the betrayal in a safe, open environment with your partner will allow for faster, more complete healing and deeper intimacy.

It is not a one-and-done occurrence.

Truth: You may need to choose to forgive repeatedly. Forgiveness is not usually a one-and-done experience. It is a process. You forgive, and then something triggers you, and you might need to forgive again. Or you forgive what you currently know to forgive or what you currently can forgive, and later there might be other aspects to forgive.

It does not mean that what he did was okay.

Intimate betrayal is never okay. What he did to you was not okay. Nothing can change that or take it away. Forgiveness is not saying that what he did was okay or that your relationship is okay. It is simply saying that he does not owe you anything anymore. Those are completely different things.

It does not mean you have to (or should) forgive immediately.

Not only do you not have to forgive immediately, but I encourage you: Don't forgive immediately or even quickly. You are not bad for taking time to grieve, honor your emotions, and grapple with the pain he has caused you. As I mentioned in Phase One, if you forgive immediately, it will stall your healing process and bury your emotions. Resist the message from anyone who tries to speed up your process or shame you for not being on their timetable.

This lack of urgency for forgiveness may make some people uncomfortable. There is often an idealized notion that you should be able to immediately forgive. To immediately get over what he did. To immediately feel okay and be ready and able to move on. This is not reality, nor is it representative of true health or healing. Is forgiveness important? Absolutely. However, all those scenarios promote an idealized fantasy of instant healing, rather than taking a breath, leaning into deep healing, and allowing everything to unfold when it is ready—which will always take longer than we'd like. So again, here in Phase Two, I encourage you to focus on your heart and holistic healing. Forgiveness will come up inside you organically if you do that. Then—and only then—is it time to forgive.

Now that I have dispelled some myths of forgiveness and identified what it is not, I want to walk you through what it is.

What Forgiveness Is

Forgiveness, first and foremost, is for you. It is about setting yourself free. It is unhooking yourself and changing how you relate to what has happened to you.

In regard to your partner, forgiveness is essentially saying that he does not owe you anything anymore. Is it fair? No. Does it free you? Yes. Forgiveness is a deep, complicated topic that each person needs to wrestle with, but I want to share with you where I landed in my forgiveness journey, in case it is helpful for you.

For me, forgiveness was acknowledging that there was nothing my husband could ever do to repay me or right the wrong he had done. So, to free myself, I chose to accept the reality of the damage it caused me, and I took responsibility to heal it myself. In the end, it was the declaration that he did not owe me anything anymore.[1]

When Do You Forgive?

As I've mentioned before, forgiveness comes after you have the truth. You need to know what you are forgiving. Forgiveness also comes after anger. You need to allow yourself time to feel the anger and wrestle with it. More than anything, though, when you are focused on your own healing and find that thoughts of forgiveness start to spring up inside of you organically, then it's time to consider forgiving.

It may go without saying, but forgiveness is for past offenses. It is not a blanket forgiveness for the future. If he relapses or does something to break your heart, safety, or trust again, then that is a new offense, and you go back to getting the truth and healing from the new offense before you focus on forgiving it.

How Do You Forgive?

Forgiveness seems straightforward until you are faced with the deep, all-encompassing pain of betrayal. Suddenly, it feels very complicated. There is no right or wrong way to forgive, but here are a few considerations to think about. First, what do you need? Do you want to give a general offer of forgiveness—a blanket forgiveness for what he has done? Or do you need to be specific and forgive each offense separately? Do you want this to be spoken or unspoken? If your partner is not emotionally safe or if he has passed away, then it may not be spoken. It is, first and foremost, for you—to free you. If you cannot share it with your partner, I recommend that you still verbalize it to someone—perhaps your therapist or a safe friend. However, if your partner is safe and you want to stay together, then I recommend expressing it to him.

1. Note: He needs to continue to do his work after you forgive him if he wants the relationship to survive and thrive. Remember—forgiving him does not make the relationship okay. He broke the relationship, so the responsibility to heal it is on him.

There is no particular method you need to use as you forgive. You can tell him, write a letter, come up with your own creative expression, or a combination of things. You get to decide. Ask yourself what you want and need. There is no right or wrong way to forgive. Ask yourself what feels like the best way to express yourself, and then go for it.

I've Forgiven Him—Now What?

I remember sitting on our brown corduroy couch in the living room after I finished reading my forgiveness letter to Nathaniel. I knew I could not do a blanket forgiveness, so I had spent hours writing out a detailed letter. I had never considered much beyond that though. At some level, I thought that by reading the letter to him—by forgiving him—I would feel relieved, sad, or perhaps closer to him. I thought I would feel . . . something. I didn't. It was rather anticlimactic, to be honest. So I went to bed, got up the next morning, and went on with life. Over the next several days, though, I felt a subtle yet profound shift inside of me. I was still mad and triggered at times. There were moments when painful memories resurfaced and I had to choose to forgive him again—but inside I had changed.

So what happens after you forgive him? You keep going. You keep leaning into your healing. You keep working through triggers when they come. You continue to honor and process through the grief when it shows up. Forgiveness is part of the process, not the end of the process. It does not resolve your pain, end your healing path, or make your relationship okay. But somehow, in the midst of everything, forgiveness shifts something deep inside you and sets your soul free.

Forgiveness is part of the process,
not the end of the process.

Layers of Impact

It's also worth noting that there may be layers of impact that unfold over time, and it's okay to take your time and notice them. These may include financial implications or how it impacts your kids or your ability to be the parent you want to be. Forgiving your partner for what he did is different from forgiving him for what it did to you.

Some women feel they have betrayed themselves by staying or by not seeing it sooner. If that resonates, you may need to spend some time and loving attention on forgiving yourself. This requires compassion and considering how you were doing the best you could in those moments.

It is also very common that your partner may not be the only one who hurt you during the process of healing from his betrayal. Many times there are additional wounds from friends, in-laws, therapists, or your faith community. These can run deep and be very wounding as well.

With any of these, the same principles of forgiveness apply. You don't need to rush into it. Notice it. Grieve it. Then, when you are ready, you can move toward forgiveness. And if you move toward forgiveness kicking and screaming, then perhaps you need to pause and focus on processing your anger and grieve more before moving forward.

Forgiving your partner for what he did is different from forgiving him for what it did to you.

Your Relationship with the World

Interacting with others becomes incredibly complicated after betrayal. As you are working through Phase Two, the feelings of shame and the desire to hide can create a sense of isolation. It is difficult to know who to tell about the betrayal, not to mention fear about how they will take it, what advice they will give, or perhaps how they will view your partner.

The temptation is to let his secret become your secret. That is understandable. Many women are concerned that they will look bad. Others are concerned that they will be judged or that people will think it is their fault. Unfortunately, the concerns of being judged are often justified. How many times have we heard some rendition of "happy men don't cheat"? The idea of dealing with what others might think of you, in addition to the pain and devastation you may already feel, may feel like too much.

Interacting with the world can suddenly feel scary, complicated, and dangerous. But I gently want to tell you that isolation is the greatest barrier to healing. We need others. We need relationships. So let me offer a few thoughts and some guidance about stepping out of isolation and back into relationships.

Telling Others

The decision of who to tell what and when is a big deal. First, you need to know that you have a right to tell others if you want to. Many women are silenced by the idea that it is their partner's story, not theirs, so they cannot tell anyone. That is not true. The moment he betrayed you and shattered your heart and everything you knew to be true, it became your story too. If he did not want others to know or to look bad in others' eyes, then he should not have broken your relationship agreement in the first place. The time to protect his reputation was before he crossed the line and betrayed you.

Him telling you to be silent and not tell others is essentially him telling you not to heal. It is also a guarantee that he will not heal and neither will the relationship. Shame grows in secrecy. If he is going to heal, then he needs to face his shame and deal with it. Of course, having said that, it is important to be thoughtful about who you tell, especially if you want the relationship to have a chance to heal.

How do you know who to tell? There is no easy answer to that question. Consider how safe you feel with the person. How have they responded in the past when you have been vulnerable or shared sensitive information? Have they kept your confidence, or did they tell others what you said? Have they told you things about others that you know they should not have?

If you are not sure how someone will respond, you can start by giving a little bit of information and observing their reaction. If they prove to be safe, perhaps you give them a little more. The fact is you will be surprised by who you can trust. Some people who you think will surely understand and be there for you may sadly disappoint you, leaving you wishing you had not told them. Then there will be others you may not expect support from who will firmly be in your corner.

You also have the right to choose not to tell people—even if they want to know. No one has a right to information about your life. You get to decide who gets to have this sensitive knowledge. You are not being fake if you choose not to tell someone or a group of people. Protecting your heart is not lying, nor is it dishonest to not share information with those who may hurt you. This includes family. If there are family members who are not safe, you do not have to tell them. Sometimes women feel that by not telling someone, they are withholding the way their partner did. It is not the same. He was betraying you. You are protecting your heart from continued fallout and damage due to his actions.

I would be remiss if I did not also prepare you for negative reactions you may get when you tell others. First, realize that everyone will probably have an opinion. Friends and family will often share their thoughts and advice out of care and concern for you, but it does not mean they are right. Be thoughtful about whose advice you take. When you find safe voices—perhaps a therapist or mentor—follow them and filter out the rest. Otherwise it will become incredibly confusing as you try to sort through the many different, often contradictory suggestions. So that you are ready when someone says something unhelpful, I recommend preparing a statement ahead of time such as "Thank you for your concern, but I don't want to talk about it right now."

Second, when you tell others, you will get varying levels of pressure for resolution. In particular, those who have not gone through a betrayal will likely have a timeline in their head of how long your pain and anger should last, when you should forgive, when you should get out of the relationship, or when you should move on and be over it. The reality is that your pain will be more intense and last longer than you or anyone else would like. Do not short-circuit your healing process or give in to the pressure to shove it down and move on. There is no timeline on healing. Take the time you need, get help, and go through the process. Give yourself the freedom to put space between you and those who are pressuring you to hurry up, move on, or get over it.

> *There is no timeline on healing.*

Third, there will be people who blame you. Society's go-to response to betrayal is to blame the one who was betrayed. It is not right or fair, but it's true. You may have people inquire into your sex life, the frequency of sex, or your availability to your partner. None of these things have anything to do with his actions. Those who don't understand intimate betrayal will be convinced they are contributing factors, but they are not. It is never your fault. If people respond in this way, you could say something like "His choices are not my fault, and I'm not interested in talking about this anymore."

Fourth, not all counselors, coaches, faith leaders, or sponsors understand how to help betrayed partners. Some will cause more harm. If you are blamed in any way, walk away. A title does not guarantee safety or expertise in healing from betrayal.

If others start to interfere with your healing process, you get to limit your interactions with them. They are not living your life nor are they in your relationship. They have no idea of the depth of your pain or the battles you are fighting. Protect your heart. Your safety matters.

Changing Friendships

Friendships will shift and change after betrayal. You will lose some. You will gain some, particularly if you lean into a support group and join a community of other women who get it. There are incredible, brave, loving, strong, compassionate women in this betrayal club that no one ever wanted to be part of. What you want and need in friendships may change as well. Many find that after betrayal, they no longer have a tolerance for lying or withholding and instead desire depth and intimacy in their friendships. That is good. It is healthy. You might go through a period of painful transition as you let go of some friendships and make new, healthier ones. If you are feeling the loneliness of that in-between place, keep going. Change is difficult, but on the other side you can have deeper, more genuine friendships.

After betrayal, there is deep beauty to discover in friendships. I lead retreats to Paris, France, for those in Phases 3 and 4 who are ready to focus on their healing and reengage with life, beauty, and adventure. Every time, I am amazed to watch a group of women transform from strangers who are isolated and alone into a beautiful, powerful community of soul sisters within a matter of days.

During one of the retreats, one of the women rolled up her sleeve to show us a beautiful tattoo of an elephant on her arm. She explained that in the wild, when a female elephant is hurt or giving birth, the other females form a tight circle around her to protect her. They stand shoulder to shoulder, facing outward to watch for danger and even kicking up dust to hide her scent from predators. That is the power of women linking arms together, and there is nothing stronger than a group of soul sisters who have gone through the hell of betrayal and are determined to rise strong together.

Being Misunderstood

Here is an unfortunate truth about healing from betrayal: You will be misunderstood. I wish that wasn't true, but it is. I wish everyone understood and honored the pain of the shattering and the strength it takes to rise and heal. The vast majority of people, however—especially if they haven't gone through it—don't get it.

People you know and love may misunderstand your emotions and decisions. Some won't understand why you stayed or why you filed for divorce. Some will think your anger is too intense, while others will think it's not strong enough. Some will think you should talk about your story more. Others will think you should get over it and not mention it again.

It feels horrible to be misunderstood or judged. It can rattle your reality and leave you grasping for a sense of truth and stability. Here's the deal though: Just because someone has an opinion and misunderstands you does not mean you are doing anything wrong. It also doesn't mean that they are right. Chances are they are not.

If you doubt yourself and feel yourself starting to spiral, reach out to the safe people who know you and can help you feel grounded, regain clarity, and reconnect with the truth about who you are. It is important to care for yourself as well. Be compassionate to yourself, and speak truth to the lies. Focus on calming your body and your nervous system so that you can feel safe in your skin again. Remember, you do not have to do this alone.

Slowing Down

In case you need to hear it, I want to offer you permission to make life smaller for a season. Dealing with the aftermath of betrayal takes every ounce of emotional, physical, and mental energy you have—and then some. Now may not be the time to launch into a new project or volunteer for the PTO at your child's school.

Think of it this way: Let's say you have ten balls of energy for the day. From those balls, you need to deal with the emotions of the betrayal, interact with your partner, parent your children, go to work, make food, and so on. How many balls of energy does the betrayal alone take from you? Clients often respond that it's taking eight to twelve balls of energy. Even if it only takes eight balls of energy, that means you have only two balls left to spend on everything else. It's an impossible situation. You will not be able to function at your normal level for a while, but that's okay. That is why it is important to cut out extra things. Now, some things will give you energy and are important to keep, but be very gentle with yourself and permit yourself to say no to things in life.

Spiritual Impact of Betrayal

I want to shift gears for a moment and talk about the spiritual impact of betrayal. Those who come from a faith background often experience a crisis of faith as a result of betrayal. Far too often, this is not met with compassion and understanding in faith communities, which leaves women even more hurt and confused. It is important to acknowledge that there are countless varieties of churches with a vast range of spiritual/religious beliefs and frameworks, so what follows here will not reflect everyone's experience. But if you have felt shamed, rejected, or betrayed by the church, or disoriented, frustrated, or disillusioned with God, then I invite you to take a moment and dive into this topic with me. As always, take what is helpful and leave the rest.

This crisis of faith often shows up in two main ways: anger at God and wounding by the church.

Anger at God

Many betrayed partners go through a period of feeling angry at God after betrayal. In fact, in one study, 46 percent of betrayed partners reported feeling anger toward God after finding out about their partner's betrayal.[2] The questions they often ask are *How could you let this happen, God?* or *Why didn't you tell me sooner?* Many women have been given the message either directly or indirectly that they would have a wonderful marriage if they did the "right" things (e.g., being gentle, attentive, and kind, serving and submitting to their husband, being sexually available at his bidding, staying at home, smoothly and efficiently running the household, or homeschooling the kids).

Then life suddenly shatters, and everything that was "supposed" to work doesn't. Instead, it turns into a nightmare, leaving them feeling betrayed and abandoned by God as well as frustrated that God didn't hold up his end of the bargain. This is profoundly disorienting. Many also feel that God goes silent at the moment they need him most—when they are trying to heal and make sense of the new reality they have been thrown into. This often results in feeling anger at God.

The reality is God understands and can take your anger. He wants to hear your heart. You are more important than your marriage, and he stands on the side of the betrayed. He would rather you wrestle with him and express your anger than walk away. He may seem silent at a time when you feel you need him the most, but hold on. He has not left you.

Wounding by the Church

Betrayed partners often feel desperate for help, safety, and comfort. Women often turn to their faith leader or faith community,

2. Crystal M. Hollenbeck and Barbara Steffens, "Betrayal Trauma Anger: Clinical Implications for Therapeutic Treatment Based on the Sexually Betrayed Partner's Experience Related to Anger after Intimate Betrayal," *Journal of Sex and Marital Therapy* 50, no. 4 (February 2024): 456–67.

who are supposed to be their safe place. Unfortunately, very often they experience even more wounding there. In fact, one study showed that faith leaders were the least helpful and most hurtful.[3] The reality is even licensed professional counselors with graduate degrees are given little to no training when it comes to helping people heal from betrayal trauma or sexual addiction, let alone pastors or faith leaders who have little to no formal training in counseling.[4] The other unfortunate reality is that many of those in church leadership are also struggling with their own sexual integrity issues. In a recent Barna study, 86 percent of pastors feel that porn use is common in Christian pastors.[5]

As a result, betrayed partners often get variations of one or both of the following messages.

It's Your Fault

The first message the church often conveys to a betrayed partner is that it's her fault either in part or in whole. This generally boils down to one of three things: you didn't have enough sex with him, you weren't attentive enough, or something is wrong with you so that he didn't feel comfortable talking to you about his struggles. This is your friendly reminder that your partner's acting out is not your fault. Ever. That was his decision. No amount of sex, attention, or talking would have made a difference. Stand tall. Just because a person has an impressive title or a position of authority does not make them right.

3. Deb Laaser et al., "Posttraumatic Growth in Relationally Betrayed Women," *Journal of Marital and Family Therapy* 43, no. 3 (July 2017): 435–47.

4. I want to pause and recognize that some faith leaders and faith communities work very hard and do provide their community members a safe place to feel broken and to heal. I want to applaud and recognize those who are out there. Unfortunately, the reality is most do not experience that, and many have been very hurt by the church. It is a gentle call to faith leaders to seek specialized training or refer out.

5. Barna Group, *Beyond the Porn Phenomenon: Equipping the Church for a New Conversation About Pornography, Betrayal Trauma, and Healing* (Barna Group, 2024), 14.

Let It Go and Be Okay

The second message a betrayed partner often hears from the church boils down to this: Let it go and be okay. In this case, the goal is to "help" you calm down, move on, and get to the place of feeling better. The heart of this message is both subtly and explicitly articulated in many different forms:

- Your anger is the problem.
- Learning to not be angry is the goal.
- He stopped and said he was sorry, so it's time to move on.
- Forgive and forget.
- You need to stay married at all costs.
- Forgiving quickly is the best way for you to heal and feel better.
- You've been angry and hurt long enough. Time's up. You need to be okay now.

The pressure is for a fast—or sometimes immediate—return to normalcy and happiness. Many faith communities want betrayed partners to be better without allowing brokenness, acknowledging their pain, or supporting them through the messy process of healing.

Spiritual Wounding

When a pastor or faith leader responds in this way, the result is spiritual wounding. Many betrayed partners end up leaving the church and struggling with their faith crisis alone. They are then fighting two battles at once: trying to heal from their partner's betrayal *and* navigating and healing from the subsequent wounds inflicted by the church. They no longer feel they belong in the system that was once their community and safety. After feeling they have already lost their partner to the betrayal, this second wounding is a profoundly isolating experience with very little guidance on how to navigate through it.

By the time a woman in this situation makes it into my office, there are layers and layers of hurt, pain, confusion, broken trust, and feelings of isolation. For those coming from conservative backgrounds, I often have to help them dig out from under false beliefs and messages before they can start to heal. The messages that left them feeling disempowered, small, silenced, and hurt include the following:

- Don't trust yourself.
- Emotions are bad.
- Boundaries are mean and selfish.
- Submit to your husband.
- Forgive immediately.
- Forgiveness is the pathway to healing.
- Just focus on the good.
- You just need to trust God and be quiet.
- Divorce should never be an option.
- God loves the marriage more than he loves you.
- Just be kind and gentle.
- You have to have sex with your partner to keep them from being tempted.
- Don't be angry.
- You are worthless except for what Jesus did for you.

These messages are often deeply ingrained within a woman's belief system, and the betrayed partner needs to reexamine them in order to find herself, her voice, and her strength to heal. If you have experienced or are working through spiritual wounding, I see you. You are not alone and it is possible to heal from this as well.

Checking In

Let's be honest. This is a lot. And it is really heavy. I picture sitting at a warm, cozy coffee shop and asking you, "So, how are you doing? How's your heart?" Then I would sip my English breakfast tea with steamed nonfat milk and listen as you talked about everything confusing, overwhelming, frustrating, and heartbreaking. I would nod along, because I've been in your shoes and sometimes all we need is a place to be heard and understood and to know that it is possible for life to be good again. To smile and laugh again. To feel peace again. I want you to know that it is true. It is possible. The road is rough with lots of twists and turns, but keep going and don't stop until you get there.

Phase Three

Realign

A New Picture

You are no longer standing helpless in the shattered pieces of your life. You have gathered them and sorted through each fragment, and the patterns are clear. Order is emerging from chaos. Colors and shapes are taking their places. You have learned to handle what was once too sharp to touch. The broken edges no longer cut you as deeply. Beauty is rising from what was broken.

Phase Three: Realign is a significant transition period, no matter what the outcome of your relationship.[1] There is no marker or event that moves you from Phase Two to Phase Three in the way

---

1. This is your friendly reminder that all are welcome here, but this section is written specifically to those in Phase Three. Some of what is written may not be applicable to you if you are in an earlier stage. You are welcome to tuck the information in the back of your mind for later, but please use discretion as you read.

151

that getting the truth moves you from Phase One to Phase Two. The shift to Phase Three happens when you realize that you have a pretty clear picture of where the relationship is headed. You then have to adjust to the new reality of your relationship and realign your life. There are three paths a relationship may take:

- **Redemption**: Your relationship is healing.
- **Roommate**: You're staying, but your relationship is not healing.
- **Divorce**: Your relationship is ending.

As we unpack each of these relationship paths, I want to remind you that you have worth and value. Period. It is not tied to the outcome of your relationship. What your partner did dramatically impacts your life, but it does not define who you are. You can heal. Joy, beauty, and adventure are possible. I know that may feel impossible, but that is exactly why I am saying it here—to keep pointing you to the light, giving you hope so you can keep going. And like I've said before, it's okay if you don't believe me. But it's true, and I will hold it for you until you are able to hold it for yourself.

7

The Redemption Path

In this chapter, we will focus on the Redemption Path. This is the path for those whose relationship is healing. This requires that you want to remain in the relationship, that your partner has done solid work over a long period of time, and that you feel safe enough to begin to reopen your heart and lean back into the relationship.

Deer in the Headlights

There's a point that I call the "deer in the headlights" moment. It is when a betrayed partner comes into my office and says—usually a bit wide-eyed and in a somewhat frightened tone—that she thinks it's time to lean back into the relationship. It's a complicated and terrifying space to be. On the one hand, it means that her partner has done enough healing and is safe enough to reengage in the relationship. That's good and usually what she has been wanting. On the other hand, leaning back into the relationship requires vulnerability and opening her heart again, which feels risky and scary.

Up until now, the way to survive after betrayal has been to set boundaries, protect her heart, and detach. Those were all vital safety measures while she watched to see if he was going to do the work and heal. He may also still be early enough in his recovery that, while hopeful, neither one of them is fully sure what will happen.

The Dilemma

How do you keep yourself safe while reopening your heart and being more vulnerable in the relationship? It is a terrifying dilemma. I want to offer a couple of practical things to consider.

Go at the pace that you feel safe. If you're opening up too soon and you're waking up at night shaking or having panic attacks, then your body is telling you to slow down. Adapt as you go. Perhaps you've been separated, and you decide to allow him back in the house. If that doesn't go well, you can change your mind and ask him to leave again. It can also be helpful to take gradual steps. For instance, if you let him move back into the house, perhaps instead of letting him move back to your bedroom, he stays in the guest room until you feel safe and see how he responds to moving home. It doesn't have to be all or nothing.

I like the analogy of putting your toe in the water. You can choose to put your toe in the water by opening up a little bit and seeing how he responds. Is he safe? Does he continue to do his work, or does he take his foot off the gas? Is he kind and empathic, or is he slipping back into anger and defensiveness? If he responds well and you feel safe, then perhaps you keep going. Watch and see what happens again. You don't have to jump all the way in right away.

If he does not respond well after you put your toe or foot in the water, then back up, regroup, and decide what your next move is. Here are some questions to ask yourself to determine if your partner is doing good healing work:

- Is he continuing to move in the direction of health and healing?
- Is he self-reflective?
- Does he see his mistakes and call himself out?
- Is he taking initiative and being proactive?
- Is he offering you his heart and sharing his emotions?
- Is he kind and empathic toward you?

Those are a few signs that indicate he is moving in the direction of healing.

Facing the Risk

Let's take a deep breath and face this head-on: Staying is risky. Opening your heart again is risky. You know all too well that there are no guarantees and that it is possible he could hurt you again. It takes courage to face these realities and bring them into the light.

I remember the day when I realized that the risk wasn't going away. That there was no guarantee my husband wouldn't hurt me again. That staying with him meant there was always a chance my heart would be shattered again. I still don't have words for the impossible tension I felt that day. *Why would I stay with someone who hurt me so badly and could hurt me again?* I asked this of our counselor, my husband, and myself. It almost felt foolish. But I loved him. I wanted to stay. I also wanted to run, hide, and protect myself. He had done such good work, but how would I ever know if that work was enough?

That was ten years ago. I did stay. He did the work. Our marriage is better than it ever was before betrayal. That does not, however, negate the fear and risk that I felt for years. Do I think he will act out again? No. Could he? Yes. Do I worry about it now? No. But does the reality that it could happen hang out in the recesses of my mind? Yes. I've made peace with that tension, and I'm able to live with it. I'm glad I stayed, but wrestling with the risk of staying is one of the most difficult things to do as a betrayed partner, particularly when you are leaning back into the relationship.

Nothing can make facing the reality of the risk comfortable, but if you know what to look for and understand the signs that he may not be going down a good path, it can help ease a little bit of the tension. Many betrayed partners struggle with this because they may not have realized their partner was acting out before, so they have little confidence they will be able to recognize it in the future. Intimate betrayal does not happen without lying and hiding, so it is very understandable that you may not have seen it. He was hiding it and probably worked hard to keep it from you.

If he betrays you in the future, is there any way to guarantee that you will see it? No. However, there are some major behavioral cues that often serve as indicators something is not okay. More specifically, if your partner's attitude or behaviors suddenly shift for the worse, or if he regresses to behaviors that were typical for him in the past when he was acting out, this is a serious red flag. These include but are not limited to the following:

- Shifting blame onto you
- Minimizing his behavior
- Getting defensive
- Verbally attacking you
- Gaslighting
- Lying by what he says or what he leaves out
- Denying
- Withdrawing

These behaviors don't automatically mean he is acting out, but they should serve as warning signs and prompt some discussions about what is going on. If you are confused or concerned, then bring it up. If there is a shift or something doesn't feel right or make sense, then express your concerns. Trust your gut. If something feels off, you have a right and a responsibility to yourself to have a conversation with him—so long as he is safe.

Allowing Your Guard to Come Down

When you are allowing your guard to come down and facing the risk of staying, safety remains very important. For most who have been betrayed, their partner was their source of safety before the betrayal. Even if he does great work and shows himself to be safe over time, it is still important that you focus on building two other sources of safety: safety in yourself and safety in community.

Safety in Yourself

The most important source of safety actually comes from within yourself. By calming your nervous system, it is possible to feel safety and peace within your body. If that sounds unbelievable, that's okay. I would have said the same thing for several years after betrayal. For now, you just need to hear that it is possible.

Calming your body and nervous system is vitally important. It is what allows you to come out of fight-or-flight mode and is the foundation for feeling safe and experiencing safety within yourself. You cannot control whether your partner is safe, but when your nervous system is at a calm baseline, it will lessen the feeling of anxiety and hypervigilance. It will also help you discern the safety of your partner's actions more clearly. When your nervous system is regulated, which means in a state of being both calm and alert—neither hyperaroused nor asleep at the wheel—you are in the best place to notice and respond.

In previous phases, caring for yourself was important to help you deal with the intensity of the crisis. In Phase Three, an ongoing self-care routine will help you deal with the inherent risk and fear associated with leaning back in. Self-care includes being gracious to yourself as you experience the emotions of this new phase of healing.

I recommend prioritizing doing things that will help your nervous system stay calm. You may need to experiment to find what works best for you, but a few ideas to consider include myofascial release, acupuncture, EMDR, and neurofeedback.

Safety in Community

We are hardwired to find safety in community. This is seen from infancy in our natural dependence on others for survival and our innate desire for attachment, and throughout life we lean on those in our innermost circle for comfort and support. When considering how to deal with the risk of staying after betrayal, a supportive community provides a unique, special, and vital role. Having people in your life who will speak the truth to you, love you no matter what, and catch you if you get knocked down provides an important layer of safety and comfort.

It is okay if you don't have that group of people dialed in. It takes intentional effort and time, but I highly recommend you make it a priority in this phase. Friendships get put on the back burner with the crisis of betrayal. When you are trying to survive and keep your head above water, there is often little time or energy to focus on friends. As you come up for air and have more emotional time and energy, though, lean back into those friendships. Consider which ones you want to keep and reach out to them. Strengthen those bonds. You may also need to be open to making new friends. The reality is we all need others.

Focus on building two sources of safety: safety in yourself and safety in community.

New Emotions

As you adjust to reengaging vulnerably in the relationship, there may be additional, more nuanced dynamics to navigate. These include softening, compassion, apologizing, relinquishing power, and hope.[1] It may feel counterintuitive to allow yourself to feel these more vulnerable states, but if your partner is doing good work and is safe, then it is a healthy and vital next step in the relationship, though it can still be scary.

I recently broke my ankle during an adventure gone wrong. Surgery, two screws, a cast, and a walking boot later, and I was good to go. My bone had healed, but I had little range of motion. I needed the protection of the cast and boot early on; I wouldn't have healed without them. But while my ankle was immobilized and healing, scar tissue had set in. In order to be able to move freely again, I had to go to physical therapy and push past everything that felt safe and comfortable. I had so much residual fear around my ankle that every session felt scary and painful, even though the bone had healed.

The Redemption Path of Phase Three feels very similar to healing after my broken ankle. All the ways you protected yourself after betrayal—detaching, setting boundaries, finding your voice—were essential, and you wouldn't have healed without them. And even though your relationship has healed enough, it can feel stiff, hard, and scary. To regain freedom, you have to have courage and gradually push past what feels scary and painful.

Softening

As your partner continues to provide safety and you lean back in, you may feel a natural pull to begin softening and may feel more tenderness toward him. That is okay. It is good. You are not

---

1. Gentle reminder: If you are reading this but you're not in Phase Three, you are welcome to tuck this information away for later, as it may not apply to you right now. Timing is important.

betraying yourself; you are giving yourself permission to be flexible and adapt as the situation calls for it. Allow yourself to feel and act on it as you are comfortable. It will take courage, but it is important. The reality is that at some level, it feels good, even right, to soften. While self-protection is the norm at this point, there is no rest there.

Compassion

In Phase Three, you may also feel more compassion for your partner. In the earlier phases, I mentioned how too much compassion for him can get you out of your shoes and into his shoes, which shuts down the healing process. In this phase, however, a gradual shift to more compassion is good and healthy. Hopefully you now feel that you have enough clarity and strength to stand on your own two feet and in your own shoes. Hopefully he has done enough work and has owned the damage he's done and is starting to better understand why he did what he did. At this point, it is safer to have compassion for him and to see life from his perspective; just be careful not to excuse his actions or lose yourself in the process.

Apologizing

Several years ago, one of the women in a support group I lead was in tears during her check-in as she shared feeling ashamed for apologizing to her partner for something she had said. She felt that by doing so, she had failed herself for not staying in her strength and power. I assured her that health and healing are not found in operating only out of her strength but also in her ability to be true to herself and honor all emotions. Allowing herself to be responsive to her emotions was a sign of health.

It is important, especially on the Redemption Path, to own when you cross a line and apologize for it. That line will look different for each person. The important thing is to stay connected with yourself, listen to your conscience, and allow yourself to soften as you lean back into the relationship.

Relinquishing Power

Power dynamics after betrayal are tricky. As I mentioned before, power is the ability to influence someone or to resist influence. In Phase Three, however, if your partner continues to be safe and you lean further back into the relationship, there will be a gradual shift toward allowing him to have more of a voice in your life again. There is a feeling of things slowly shifting to a healthy relational balance. You can receive his influence and feedback without letting it define your worth or allowing him to make your decisions for you. In this way, you maintain your autonomy while also leaning into connection with him.

Hope

Hope can feel like a four-letter word after life blows up. Hope is important in everyone's life, but after betrayal, it can feel scary and vulnerable. Allowing yourself to feel hope opens you up to getting hurt. In this phase, however, you may feel hope rising up more, and I encourage you to open your heart to it. Embrace hope and welcome it back into your life, even if tentatively.

Holding Opposite Emotions

Part of healing is expanding your ability to hold emotions and realities that are seemingly contradictory and conflicting. The tension of hope and fear is a perfect example. Another example is the tension of simultaneously holding both joy of the present and sadness of the past. It can feel incredibly complicated to laugh and smile with the one who caused you such grief and pain. It can be true that you want to open your heart and move closer to him and at the same time run away from him. Holding opposite emotions is part of the complexity of healing. It may be uncomfortable and confusing, but it is real. It takes you to a new depth. Allow it to grow and expand you.

One of the most difficult and important dichotomies to hold is the realization that your partner has the capacity for both great good and great evil. Both are true. And that is the case for all humanity, but there is nothing quite like betrayal to make you face it head-on. Wrestling with and accepting that reality—even though it is uncomfortable—is an important part of healing.

When He's "Further Along"

As you and your partner continue to heal, there may come a point in time when it feels as if he is further along in the process than you are. If so, that does not mean you are doing anything wrong. It may mean that he is doing really good work. That's great. Remember, he was aware of his actions all along, which gives him a leg up in the healing process. He did not have to deal with the shock of discovery, shattering of his worldview, or trauma to heal from. Take your time and heal at your own pace.

It is also not uncommon to feel that since he is further along in his healing, you are now at fault for somehow holding the relationship back. I want to pause here and remind you that the reason the relationship had to heal in the first place was because of what he did. You are not a problem, and you are not hurting the relationship by taking the time you need to heal.

There are a few things to watch for in this scenario. First, if he starts to hold his progress over you, then that is an indication he is not as far along as he thinks he is. He needs to be kind, patient, and humble if he wants you to feel safe enough to open your heart back up to him. Second, there are many ways to get stuck in this process. If you feel stuck, it may help to reach out to a counselor who specializes in this area, who can help get you moving again. There is no shame in being stuck or getting help. You get to own your journey and do what you need to do for your healing.

Respect, Trust, and Attraction

Many betrayed partners struggle with not respecting, trusting, or feeling attracted to their partner early on in the Redemption Path. It is common for my clients to ask if they will ever feel those things again. Yes, those feelings can grow and return with time. They are not, however, things to focus on or run after. They come with healing, safety, and connection. If he is doing the work to own his decisions by being humble, trustworthy, and empathic, then those feelings can emerge over time. You cannot get them by pursuing them directly though. They are by-products of healing.

More Freedom, Less Freedom

As the two of you continue to grow and heal, you may find that you experience more freedom in some areas of your relationship than you did before the betrayal. For instance, you may feel more freedom to express your emotions with your partner. The two of you may develop a deeper intimacy and greater authenticity than you have ever experienced before.

There may also be areas of life where you experience less freedom. For instance, perhaps you felt very free while having sex before, and now you are more reserved or have sworn off lingerie. Or perhaps you feel less free around your friends or family because they did not support you through the pain in the way you hoped they would.

There is a natural recalibration that happens as the crisis calms and you come up for air. There will be unexpected joys and gains—along with sorrows and losses. As you feel comfortable, share your observations, thoughts, and feelings with your partner. Some areas heal more quickly than others, so be patient and go at the pace you feel comfortable with.

8

The Roommate Path

The second relationship path in Phase Three is the Roommate Path. This is when you decide to stay in the relationship, but it is clear that your partner is not fully doing the work. He may be doing some work and recovery activities but is continuing to break your relationship agreement or has not done the character work needed to really empathize and connect with you.

There are many reasons why women choose to stay in relationships that are not serving them. Many cannot support themselves financially or don't want their children to go through a divorce. Others feel trapped in an abusive relationship or believe it is wrong for them to divorce. If you are in this situation, I want to surround you with compassion and understanding that you are making the best decision you can for yourself and your family in this moment.

The truth is that this is perhaps the most misunderstood, overlooked, isolated, and judged group of betrayed partners. People understand when a relationship either heals or ends in divorce. There are empathy and encouragement and plenty of support groups to help them as they heal. Not so with those who stay, even though his growth and their relational healing have not occurred. As one woman put it, "No one knows what to do with us."

No Shame in Staying

Many women on the Roommate Path feel a deep sense of shame for staying. No one starts a relationship thinking that betrayal will be part of it. And if you considered the idea that it could happen one day, then chances are you promised yourself that if it ever did, you would leave. Then it happens, and the decision is no longer as clear as you thought it would be. Perhaps you think, *Well, it only happened once, and everyone makes mistakes,* or *The kids are having a hard time and need stability.* Maybe you got pregnant before finishing college and never got your degree, so you don't have a way to financially support yourself and your kids. Perhaps due to religious beliefs you think that divorce is not an option.

Let's be clear: There is no shame in staying. There are many real and legitimate reasons to stay. The reality is, though, that staying comes at a cost. That cost is you. And again—zero shame. Choosing to stay now also doesn't mean you can't or won't make a different choice later. Things can change with time or with more information, support, and resources. But for the moment, I want to offer deep compassion. Staying when he is not doing the work is one of the most difficult—and sometimes the only—decision you can make.

Reasons for Staying

There are four main reasons why women decide to stay or feel trapped and unable to leave: finances, kids, abuse, and conditioning.

Finances

A common reason women feel trapped and cannot leave a relationship is that they do not have the finances to support themselves (and their children, if they have them and they are still at home). It may be that they don't have the education they need to get a job that pays well, or they have been out of the workforce for a time and don't have an income or an immediate job opportunity available. Some women don't have access to the family finances, which prevents them from having the information needed to make a decision. All this can leave women feeling incredibly powerless.

If this is your situation, then information is power. If you don't have access to the family finances right now, you can start by gathering information. You can contact the bank and create your own login for the accounts you are using. You can also request a copy of your past tax returns and learn a lot from the information within those documents. Remember, the family finances belong to you as well, even if you are not working outside of the home.

I encourage you to fight the potential overwhelm and move into action. Start gathering data. If you did decide to leave, how much money would you need to live? What types of jobs are available to you right now? If you need to go back to school, what would that look like? Are there loans available to cover your schooling and living expenses?

Taking steps to learn about your finances and consider your needs and options does not necessarily mean you are going to leave, but it is important you have the information you need to make informed choices.

Kids

Many women stay in difficult situations because they are concerned about the impact a divorce would have on their kids. They don't want to disrupt the family unit or cause trauma for their children. Perhaps they don't want to have to go back to work and lose time with their kids. Maybe they don't want to risk the potential of their kids having a less-than-desirable stepmom in the future.

Regardless, some women prioritize having an intact family unit for the sake of their kids, even at a high personal cost.

I want to honor what an impossible decision that is when you feel like you are holding your shattered heart in one hand and your kids' hearts in the other. There is often a silent acceptance of the idea, *I don't matter. I'll let my heart die if that's what it takes to keep my kids' hearts beating.* There is this idea that your voice doesn't matter—that your wants, needs, and happiness don't matter. The danger with accepting that message is that it can lead to your inner light dimming and going out.

If you are staying for the kids' sake, it is important to be careful how you communicate that with them. You don't want to inadvertently put them in the middle or for them to feel responsible for you being in a hurtful or emotionally harmful situation. If your kids are old enough, talk to them and ask them how they are doing with the family situation. Get curious about their hearts, how they are feeling, what they are worried about, or questions they may have.

To expand your understanding of what is possible, it may also be helpful to talk to others who have gone through similar situations, or read helpful and impactful books. There are no easy answers or quick solutions to these dilemmas. Again, be very gentle with yourself. Though your family situation did not turn out how you wanted it to, healing is possible for you and your kids.

Abuse

Some women stay in the relationship because of abuse. As mentioned earlier, research shows that abuse, in its various forms, is present in a lot of relationships where there is betrayal. A betrayed partner may be scared to leave the relationship for fear of retaliation. The betrayer may have also beaten down his partner's view of herself to such a degree that she thinks she is not capable of living without him or that no other man would ever want her. Being in an abusive relationship is a serious and dangerous situation. It complicates everything and requires specialized help by qualified professionals.

Conditioning

Another reason women stay in unhealthy relationships, particularly when their partner is not doing great work, is because of conditioning. Conditioning is the spoken and unspoken messages women receive about their value and role in the world and in relationships. Often these messages are so ingrained that you may not even realize they are driving your decisions and the way you view yourself.

Conditioning messages may sound something like this: Women are supposed to always nurture and take care of others. Your needs, wants, and desires are not as important as those of others and are not a priority.

For those who come from certain faith communities, the messages get even more constraining:

- Don't be angry.
- Don't trust your emotions.
- Submit to your husband.
- Don't think too highly of yourself.
- Your value comes from being married, having kids, and serving others.
- Don't question authority.
- Boundaries are bad.
- Women are not as valuable as men.
- Anything empowering women is bad.
- God hates divorce.

It is important to recognize the messages that you were given, so you can choose which beliefs you'd like to keep and which ones you'd like to leave behind. Know that changing these core beliefs and conditioning messages will take time and attention, so be gentle with yourself as you recognize when they surface and as you start to learn different ways of thinking and responding.

Impact of Staying

While emotions are strong and important throughout the healing process after betrayal, the Roommate Path brings with it a new and nuanced set of emotions—another layer of grieving. It is a loss, or even death, of hope. A resignation. It's no longer that betrayal is part of your story—now it simply *is* your story. Or that's how it feels unless something dramatic occurs. Confusion, resigned disbelief, bitterness, loss of voice, and isolation are normal emotions that wax and wane on this path. Numbing out to protect yourself from feeling seemingly unsolvable emotions is also common.

There are a few hidden consequences of staying in the relationship when he is not doing good work. The first is the potential for your inner light to dim or go out. The second is the impact on your body. While most betrayed partners feel these consequences to varying degrees, those on the Roommate Path are impacted more significantly.

This is the population of women I am most concerned about because I think the absolute greatest tragedy after betrayal is when a woman's light dims and she loses herself. This is the group I see it happen to most often. The idea of someone's light dimming is when they slowly, over time, begin to lose themselves. Excitement slowly fades to indifference. Anger gives way to numbness. Connections shift to isolation. Dreams are erased and hope is eradicated. Women often describe this as "becoming a shell of who I once was." It is when shutting down feels like the only way to survive.

The other hidden impact of staying is the way it affects the body. The trauma of betrayal floods your body with stress hormones as your brain signals your body into fight-or-flight mode. The problem is that if the stress never resolves and you are constantly being sent back into fight-or-flight mode by your partner's continued actions, it significantly wears on your body. Your body is not meant to live with such high levels of stress hormones for prolonged periods of time, and eventually the stress can cause physical problems such as cardiovascular disease, autoimmune disorders, and even cancer, as the data from the HAB survey previously showed.

Minimizing the Impact

It doesn't have to be this way though. Your light doesn't have to go out. But in order to prevent yourself from numbing out or shutting down, you need to shift focus and find where you can take action. Focus on your physical health. Go to your doctor appointments. Perhaps hire a nutritionist or a personal trainer to get your body healthy and strong. Refuse to allow yourself to slip away. Fight it. Make time for yourself. Join that community theater or pickleball league. This is your one life to live.

It doesn't stop there though. Emotions still need to be processed in order to heal. Reach out to a counselor or go to a support group for women going through similar things, and get the emotions out of you. Talk them out. Cry them out. Scream them out as you're driving in the car. Beat them out in a smash room. Hire a massage therapist to massage them out. Remember, it's not just your emotions at stake but also your physical health. Those emotions need to get out of your body.

Find places where you can take action.

Emotional Divorce

Just as there is no one right path to healing after betrayal, there is no one right path to staying either. There is no manual, and there is no right or wrong. However, if you choose to stay and you want to protect your health and prevent your light from dimming, then there will have to be an incredible amount of detachment. I'd like to introduce you to a woman who beat the odds and was able to stay in the marriage and still thrive by emotionally divorcing her husband. To this day, she remains legally married and in the home with her husband and their son, but she is emotionally divorced.

Meet Amber.[1] She is a kind, strong, self-aware, and empowered woman who beat the odds of staying and thriving. I thought I would let her share how she did it. She is not offering the "right" way. I just want you to hear that it is possible. So grab a cup of coffee, wrap yourself in a fuzzy blanket, and listen in as I interview her.

Amber smiled as I opened the door and she made her way into my office. She had a calm, relaxed energy about her—the kind that characterizes someone who is deeply comfortable in her own skin. As we got settled, we chatted easily about the upcoming holidays and her son's activities. I positioned the microphone next to her but far enough out of the way that it would not distract from our conversation. I thanked her for being willing to share her story and give other women hope that it is possible to stay and not simply survive but thrive. Then, as I often do, we jumped into the deep end and got down to the topic.

Amber, you said that you decided to stay and live with your husband. You are still legally married, but you are essentially emotionally divorced. Is that true?

Yep.

1. The person's name and identifying details have been changed or presented in composite form to ensure privacy, safety, and anonymity.

How did you come to that decision?

For a long time after D-Day, I could not stand to be near him. There was a slight ease during the day when he was gone, and then as soon as time started getting closer to him coming home, I could feel the tension build. As soon as I heard the garage door go up, I would clench with anger. Him walking in the door . . . I would be trying to hold on to myself so that I don't wind up in jail or yell in front of our son. It got to the point where I was like, *Okay, I see how I'm reacting. I see how bad this is.* And at that point, it felt like I had very little control over it. So I decided that I needed to be away for a while. Number one, just to give myself a break. Number two, see what it was like to be a single mom. Number three, to prove my strength to myself.

During that time, I would have panic attacks thinking about divorce. I knew he wasn't going to do it, so if it's going to happen, I have to initiate that paperwork. I knew that it wasn't my fault, but I would be the one finalizing the separation of our family.

I realized that if I filed for divorce, he would be free. If I signed that paper, he could go find anybody to marry. And I then have to share my son with that person. So, could I trust him to go out and find somebody who's going to have my son's best interests at heart when he's not with me? Am I willing to share holidays? Am I willing to share everything?

No.

So I decided that I needed to stay, and if I did that, I had to work. I knew that it would be very hard, but I had to try as hard as I could to figure out myself because I knew I couldn't figure him out. I couldn't change him, but I've got to figure out me so that I can stay in the marriage—in the house—and keep my son's life as stable as possible. That became my biggest driving force.

I remember asking my therapist, "Do you think I can pull this off? Do you think there's any chance that I can pull this off?" I really wanted to hear, "No problem. You got this!" But instead, he said, "It is possible, but I've never seen it done."

I remember taking that in and allowing myself the grace to fail if I couldn't do it, because I couldn't do superhuman things. But I decided that I had to try. I knew that having a safe family structure, security, and the foundation of knowing he had a mom and a dad was incredibly important for my son. I knew that if I wanted to try to keep that intact, I'd have to get my stuff together.

I hear you say that in order to be able to stay in the marriage with your husband—who wasn't doing the work to heal—you'd have to focus on yourself. But what did that look like? What did you mean when you said that you had to get your stuff together?

First, I had to do a lot of shedding. It was shedding the burden that society, family, and trauma had placed on me, as well as some that books, podcasts, and therapists had placed on me. It was shedding all of that and getting rid of what I'm not, to make space to say, *Well, who am I, and who do I want to be?*

The fear of letting my son down was the fuel that kept me going. It was the motivation to keep looking, to keep trying. Knowing that I still needed more tools. Things like meditation, exercise, journaling, and coming to recognize the places where fear had stopped me, where old beliefs stopped me, and then figuring out what I can do to move through and get past this.

Slowly, over time, there were fewer panic attacks and less negativity. There was a little more sunshine every day. And I very intentionally focused on figuring out what I wanted and needed. I would sometimes stop for several minutes to try to figure out what sounded good to me. Then, I'd make an intentional journey to seek it and find it. I realized I didn't have to wait for it to come to me or hope that somebody else will give it to me. I could make it happen.

What about the marriage? Was there a moment that shifted your focus from working on the marriage to realizing he was not changing, and taking care of yourself?

Yeah, it was several years ago. We were at Chipotle for lunch. He grabbed a table, and I got in line to order. As I waited, I looked back and saw him checking out a beautiful college girl a few tables away. He couldn't take his eyes off her. And I thought, okay, how many counselors have we been to? How many thousands of dollars have we spent on help? The time, the tears, the agony, the begging, the pleading, the *please understand me, please see my hurt, please come help me, please.* And this is where we are at? And so I thought, okay, this is it. I had to face the fact that he was not changing.

That was when I said, okay, I need to start emotionally distancing. I can't keep doing this. It hurts too much to have hope every morning, but also the knowing that I'm going to get hurt every day.

What did that look like for you to start to emotionally distance yourself?

I realized that I needed a safe space. But how in the world do you have a safe space when you live with the father of your child? And so I told him, "It is time for you to leave the room. This is my bedroom. I need this space."

I had to set boundaries, like this is my car and that is your car. And when I go places, I'm going to take this car. When you go places, you're gonna take that car. When we go as a family, then what are we gonna do? Then try to figure out that middle ground.

I wound up making a new group of friends. He came to a few events, and finally I said, "You can't come. These are my friends. I made these friends. I feel safe with them. I am developing a new part of my life, and you're not allowed in this part." So now I think I can say that I have emotionally divorced my husband.

What does it look like at home?

He has his room. I have my room. We try to have dinner together as a family several nights a week. The three of us go skiing together in the winter. If my son has a track meet or choir concert, we go together. We talk about parenting stuff, but that's about it. I have no idea what goes on with his job. And he has no idea what is going on in my life. We've worked hard to still be friends or at least be able to interact. That has been my goal. I want our son to see as little weirdness in our family as possible.

Does he still check out other women?

Yeah.

Does it still hurt?

Yes, sometimes it does. It comes in as a reminder that I'm still not enough. And I have to stop myself and say, *No, this has nothing to do with me.* And I have my strategies. If I can walk ahead of him, I do that. That way I don't even pay attention. Depending on how well I'm taking care of myself, it can be a lot easier or a lot harder to say that it is about him—*it has nothing to do with me.* And it still hurts. I haven't figured out a way to 100 percent lift that feeling and just give it to him. But I know how to sit in the hurt now. I know that the hurt will subside. And I know that there is immense joy and magic in this world. I can continue to look at him and his dysfunction, or I can turn and I can look over here, and I can look at all the things that I can succeed at—that I do have control over—that I can be happy and joyous about. It's okay for me to put aside the yucky and purposefully seek out the good.

If I want to be the person that I really want to be, then I need to be a person with as much love, compassion, and strong boundaries as I possibly can. And in the situation where we are all three in the same house, we all benefit. And that is hard to swallow because, once again, he screwed up. He didn't do the work. But we all have more together, and I definitely believe that it is beneficial for my son.

What encouragement do you have for betrayed partners who are in this situation?

It can be done. It is not easy, and it is different. It's not for everybody, and there are painful moments, but it can be done.

There are no books on this. There is no pathway for this. There's no support for this. I still keep very, very much hidden the details of what has happened because it's so easy for other people to say, "Divorce him! He's a scumbag." That can mess with my mind and the confidence that I have built. I have to find the courage to venture out away from any conventional path or way of thinking and literally forge my own path to get there. If you are on this path, you may need to do that as well.

But you have to start. It'll be messy, and that's okay. If you make a choice and it takes you in the wrong direction, that's okay too. Don't stop. Try something else. If it's not quite right, adjust.

I'm proud of my new life. It was imagined by me, designed by me, created by me, defended by me, and nourished by me.

It can be done.

9

The Divorce Path

ivorce is a trauma unto itself. It is not merely the legal dissolution of a marriage; it is the unraveling of a shared life, the loss of dreams once held together. And for many, it's a journey of survival and rebirth.

Of all the women I've worked with who ended up getting divorced, very few actually wanted their marriage to end. They wanted their partner to do the work, but when he didn't, they eventually needed to move forward with divorce to save themselves.

However you ended up on this path . . . I'm sorry. Whether you filed immediately or fought for years, hoping your marriage would survive . . . I'm sorry. Whether he gave up and walked away, or you filed yourself . . . I'm sorry. Every scenario ends in pain and loss, and no one signs up for a relationship with this as the goal. But I want you to know that there is a good life ahead for you. This is not the end; it is an interruption to the plot, but there is still a good story to be written.

Not only can you heal, but one of the strongest findings about healing that came out of my HAB survey concerns divorced women.

More specifically, betrayed partners who get divorced reported significantly higher trust in themselves compared to those who stay in the relationship. If you are divorced or facing the Divorce Path, I want you to know this is just one of the ways there is healing and personal redemption for you.

I want to pause and acknowledge that betrayed partners who get divorced are often left out or ostracized. The switch from fighting for your marriage to divorcing can be a jarring and lonely transition. Suddenly, the groups you belonged to no longer fit, and you are now a soon-to-be single living in a couples' world—which can be overwhelming at best and terrifying at worst.

I have walked alongside dozens of women who have found themselves, for one reason or another, on the Divorce Path. At the same time, I want to acknowledge that I have not personally gone through divorce. So here I can lead from a place of professional experience but am limited in my personal experience. Fully aware of this limitation and with the desire to give you the critical and expert support you deserve, for this chapter I have interviewed and consulted with many amazing women who have gone through divorce with the hope that you will truly feel seen and heard in these pages.

Contrary to what you may often feel "out there," *you belong here*. This book is for all betrayed partners, no matter the outcome of your relationship. You are seen and heard . . . and you are important.

Should I Stay or Should I Go?

Clients often ask me when they will know if they should stay or go. At that point, I usually pick up my calendar and start flipping through it as if to pick a date. It usually breaks the tension and the seriousness of the situation long enough for us to look at each other and smile. The reality is we both know there is no right answer to that question. It is a very fair and valid question, but no one can—or should—answer it for you.

I encourage you to find a compassionate therapist who won't tell you what decision to make but will help you see that you are worthy of whatever choice is right for you. If you were in my office right now, sitting on one of my soft, tan chairs, I'd tell you that you deserve to be treated with love and respect. You have a choice: You can stay, or you can leave. Both are options. And I'd probably sound like a broken record as I look into your eyes and tell you that you have great worth and value.

Divorce is a trauma unto itself.

It is helpful to have a counselor reflect back on your beauty and strength, especially if you are not able to see it for yourself yet, someone to walk beside you as you try yet another couples' counselor or come into the office after your partner relapses again. You may need to hear many times over that your partner's betrayal is not okay, you deserve better, and you have not failed if you get divorced. It is also helpful to have support as you start to step into your strength, find your voice, and believe that you get to set boundaries and create your life.

When it comes to making a decision, no one gets to make that call except for you because no one is going to live with the reality of it except for you. There can be a lot of pressure from the outside to resolve the tension. You have every right to make a decision at any point in time, but I encourage you to give yourself the grace and freedom to take as much time as you need.

Here's what I've seen: You'll know when it's time. There is a shift that happens in women when they've hit the end. There is usually a settledness that comes with feeling like they have done everything they could do. That is not without perhaps fear or sadness, but usually there remains a strong sense that it's time and the relationship is truly done.

Some women express shame for staying so long, but the reality is that it takes as long as it takes to be ready and to know that it's the right choice for you. If that means it takes six months, a year, or ten years, that's okay. It may be helpful to find people who understand and respect this process. It's also okay to thank others for their concerns but to let them know that you are not open to talking with them about your relationship.

Preparation Period

You may know that it's time to be done long before you are actually ready to take action or file paperwork. This is common and especially important when it comes to preparing financially and assessing where your kids are at (if you have them and they are still at home). You may want to get finances in order first, finish your schooling, strengthen your relationship with your kids, get them through the school year, or work on getting stronger before you are ready to face the reality of the divorce process. There is wisdom in allowing yourself a preparation period. Take whatever time you need to be strong and prepared before taking final action.

Financial Survival

One of the main things that traps women in unhealthy relationships is finances. Money is a silent but powerful weapon in many intimate partnerships, and it is obviously an issue in many divorces as well. Many women are financially dependent on their partners. Perhaps they decided to stay home with their kids and didn't finish college, or maybe they left a career behind.

For others, their partner made enough money that they did not need to work and decided not to. In many relationships, there is a natural division of labor. What at first may have seemed like a helpful move—giving the role of financial manager to their partner—may have inadvertently resulted in being shut out of any knowledge or control of their money. In addition, legal fees, division of assets, and the cost of child support and alimony leave many women fearful at best and frighteningly compromised at worst.

If you are considering or facing divorce, it is very important to get as much information as you can. There are several things to consider that may help ease the transition:

- What accounts do you have? Do you have access to them? How much money is in them? As I mentioned before, if you do not know or are blocked from this information, you can request a copy of your last tax return and get valuable information from that.
- How does your state view the division of assets, child support, and spousal support? You may want to schedule a free consultation with an attorney to get the information you need and to understand your rights.
- How easily can you access employment so that you have income to support yourself? How much schooling do you need? Can you start that now? Do you need to update your résumé and brush up on interviewing skills? Would your current job allow you to increase your hours if needed?

If you are able, consulting with a financial adviser can be very helpful. There are some who even specialize in helping women going through divorce.

The Court System

When you engage in the court system, it's important to know that it is a very different ball game and it plays by a very different set of rules. Unfortunately, the court system is not trauma informed, and the main drive is to reach a resolution through negotiation. The fact that your partner betrayed you usually bears little to no weight in court. I highly recommend that you get specialized help from those who know and understand the legal system to help you navigate the process.

I also want to recognize the reality that divorce and the court process can make you feel like the ground is falling out from underneath you. The reality is that you lose so much in divorce. You lose time with your kids. You lose the ability to influence who is around them and if another woman becomes their stepmom. You lose holidays, birthdays, and bedtimes. You lose income and assets. You may lose financial stability. You may lose the ability to stay in your home and have to start over in an apartment. You may lose the option to go to counseling and get the help you need. The fact is you have to start over in so many ways.

The divorce process brings up a lot of emotions, and the court process amplifies them—feelings of being powerless, misunderstood, alone, angry, scared, blamed, overwhelmed, sad, hurt, and judged, to name a few. If any of those emotions resonate with you, know that it is normal. Many women also struggle with thoughts of *Did I fail? Was it my fault?* or the nagging thought, *No one will ever want me again.* While all the emotions and fears make sense, it doesn't mean they are true. Consider whose voice is really in your head. Are these things your ex-partner has said . . . or perhaps an abusive parent? Evaluate whether they are messages you want to allow in or if you need to speak truth to the lies and fight back.

Women who have gone through the court system and experienced the loss of control over many significant parts of their life find that focusing on what they can control is helpful and grounding.

That may include redefining what success looks like. For instance, success might be as simple as staying connected to yourself during the court proceedings. Perhaps it is choosing to take a walk to calm your nervous system before your hearing starts. Maybe it is choosing radical acceptance even though a ruling is not fair or right. Fight the powerlessness by focusing on things within your control.

Meet Julie.[1] She navigated betrayal, divorce, and the court system and has now created a beautiful, fulfilling life for herself and her kids. When I asked her how she took control of her life after divorce, she shared this:

> I did many things that helped me feel a sense of strength and agency. I learned to make meaningful traditions with my kids—whether keeping ones we had or creating new ones—and being present so I could make the most of the time I do have with them. I redecorated rooms in my house that held painful memories and turned them into rooms that are now a sanctuary for me. Financially, I focused on what I can control regarding my work and rebuilding my financial stability. It gave me such a sense of power and strength to create financial freedom for myself.
>
> While initially the shock and adjustment were really painful, I was able to build a really beautiful life by focusing on what I could control within my new reality. It felt incredibly grounding to rebuild my life that way. It was a series of a lot of small steps, but I eventually got to a place where I felt agency and joy . . . even though I am living in this new reality.

Grief and Mourning

Divorce is a whole new grieving process. The grief of betrayal is huge by itself, but when you add the death of the marriage on top

---

1. The person's name and identifying details have been changed or presented in composite form to ensure privacy, safety, and anonymity.

of that, it is even more significant. All that you've learned from earlier chapters still applies: the stages of grief, honoring your emotions, and being gentle with yourself. Grief is often prolonged with divorce . . . not simply because there is more to grieve but also because the energy and logistics of divorce demand time and attention. Grief about everything you've gone through—*and are going through*—can get pushed to the back burner at times. That is okay, but you may need to be intentional about setting time to allow yourself to grieve so your healing doesn't get lost in the midst of everything else that is going on. Counseling and journaling can be very helpful. Try to listen to your heart and body and follow their lead on what needs attention next.

While *grief* is the internal processing of loss, it can also be helpful to incorporate *mourning*, which is the external and even public processing of grief, often done with others. One example of mourning is the public expression of grief at a funeral or a celebration of life service. Mourning after divorce allows you to acknowledge the good and bad of what you lost and gives you a sense of control regarding closure. This could take many different forms. You could invite your support group over and have a service for the death of your marriage. If you are more in the anger phase, then perhaps you go to a smash room with others and physically move the energy out of your body in that safe environment. Maybe you'll want to hold a bonfire ceremony and burn your wedding pictures. The goal is to mark the closure—the death—of the relationship in a way that is meaningful to you and done in the presence of supportive people.

Divorce is a whole new grieving process.

Community and Support

Divorce not only impacts the marriage—it impacts friendships, family dynamics, community involvement, and sociocultural traditions. The shift to being a single person in a couples' world can be extremely difficult. Many experience the loss of relationships for any number of reasons. Friends may not be supportive of divorce or understand the reasons for this decision. Couple friends may fade away. You may be shunned by your family or faith community. And the holidays can be very painful.

Divorce requires an overhaul of your social world, but here's a secret that many women will attest to: You will lose some friends, and what you need in friendships will change, but there are incredible people waiting for you on the other side. The women who don't just survive but thrive on the other side of divorce are those who lean hard into finding and developing new friendships and new, healthy communities that fit them *now*. These can come in many forms, including divorce care groups, book clubs, retreats, community theater, special interest groups, faith communities, or any number of creative spaces. They are out there. It will take time and energy to develop these, but it will be worth it.

Beyond that, you will need a support network. It's important to reach out when you need help. As one divorced mom put it, "Get comfortable with asking for what you need. Be okay with recognizing your limitations and then finding resources to fill those needs." Start by identifying what your needs are. They may include help with the house, childcare, preparing freezer meals, or budgeting, to name a few. Then brainstorm about which people in your life already have these particular skill sets and ask if they would be willing to help you. You may also need to add professionals to your team, such as a counselor or coach who can help you navigate life. Perhaps you need a counselor for your kids as well as they deal with their own grief and the many changes.

Each person's needs for a support network will look different, so make it work for you.

"Get comfortable with asking for what you need."

Hope

Remember, there is a good life ahead. Divorce is not the end of your story. It's the end of the marriage, but there is more ahead for you. There is hope. You can heal. You can rebuild and create a beautiful life. Remember that divorced women had significantly more trust in themselves than other groups surveyed. That did not magically happen. No . . . they were in the trenches. They wrestled with pain, sadness, imperfect societal systems, and tough social and familial dynamics—and continued adjusting through it all. And somewhere along the way, that trust in themselves started to grow . . . and it can for you too. Keep going.

Phase Four

Rebuild

Your Mosaic Masterpiece

One by one, the broken pieces you chose to keep have been artfully placed, rearranging your life into a new design. Those fragments have formed something entirely new—a beautiful design with an array of patterns, sparkling with color. It is a reflection of you, the new you.

You are no longer broken. You are brave.

No matter what path your relationship took, all betrayed partners come back together in Phase Four: Rebuild. This is where the focus shifts from healing the relationship with your partner to healing yourself. There are, of course, aspects of this self-healing that happen along the way, but this is the phase where you have an increased capacity to harness your empowerment and more fully engage the process of rebuilding your sense of self: unearthing lost parts of yourself, discovering new aspects of yourself, and after everything you have worked through, reclaiming joy and even adventure. This phase may also include rediscovering who you are after betrayal, forming new friendships, forgiving yourself, regaining your physical, emotional, and financial well-being, and dealing with lingering wounds and scars, to name a few.

And as wonderful as all this may sound—and, of course, it is wonderful—it is also quite the endeavor. You may feel overwhelmed at times, but it *can* be done. The important thing here is to pause and take stock of where you are and where you want to go. You now have the sacred responsibility to build a life and future that you are excited to live.

10

(Re)Discovering You

There is an organic shift that happens after the crisis of the relationship has settled. You feel that your head is finally above water long enough to catch your breath, and the focus moves away from your partner and the relationship and onto you.

At this point, clients often say, "It's time to focus on me" or "I need to focus on myself and heal." While aspects of healing may have occurred throughout the journey, it becomes the primary focus in Phase Four.

It can be scary the first time you have enough air to come up and look around. Whether the relationship made it or not, it is a new, unknown world. What will your life look like now? How do you create a new life from the ashes of betrayal? You may have been thrown backward financially, emotionally, psychologically, or physically.

Where do you start? Is it possible to find the strength you need after all you have already gone through? It can feel too hard, too much, and too overwhelming.

It can be hard to see the light when you are buried under so much. But as someone who is looking at the full picture and has walked hundreds of other women through this process, I want to encourage you that it is possible to heal and create a life you are excited to live. It is hard, but you can do hard things. You have overcome so much already, and you can make it through.

You can heal and create a life you are excited to live.

Surveying the Damage

As you start this next phase of healing and designing your future, it is important to first take a little time and survey the damage. Pause long enough to honor all the things you lost along the way because of betrayal. It is also important to recognize the things you have gained. Those can be harder to see or recognize, but each one of them is hard-earned and deserves to be honored. You can be proud of them without having to be thankful for the trauma that brought them about.

For me, there were certainly a lot of losses, but there were also many solid gains. I found my voice. I came out knowing that I am strong at the core of my being—not despite what happened but because of it. I discovered a creative, entrepreneurial part of me that I didn't know existed. I will never be grateful that I experienced betrayal, but I am proud of who I have become.

What about you? If you need help identifying your gains and losses, ask yourself the following questions:

- What did I lose?
- What do I miss?
- What do I want to leave behind?
- How have I changed?
- In what ways am I proud of myself?

Taking Steps

You have one life to live. From here forward, you get to make it what you want. That does not mean you can control your partner, erase what happened, or ignore the impact of his decisions. It does mean, however, that you can chart a course and walk forward despite all that life has thrown at you.

As you move forward in reclaiming your life, know that it will take time. When you start to come up for air after betrayal, it is very tempting to fall into one of two extremes—getting overwhelmed and shutting down or wanting to conquer everything all at once. I suggest that you pick one aspect of life you want to reclaim and focus on that. Every aspect takes mental and emotional energy—not to mention time and money. It may not be possible to get on top of finances, finish a degree, and lose twenty pounds all at once. Pick one, focus on it, and patiently move forward.

For example, if the most pressing thing for you is to get on top of your finances, then gently put all the other things on hold and focus on finances. Once that is under control and you have more time, along with more mental and emotional energy, then you can move on to the next thing on your list.

Be very gentle with yourself. Take it slowly and remember that you don't need to be perfect. Just take one step at a time.

Healing the Relationship with Yourself

Here's a secret: In the long run, your relationship with yourself is the most important and valuable aspect of healing. According to the participants of the HAB survey, 91 percent of betrayed partners felt they had lost parts of themselves after betrayal. Some felt that the best part of them was dead and that they would never get her back. The reality is she's still there. She's just buried and waiting for you to come find her.

Taking stock of how betrayal has impacted your relationship with yourself is important. Ask yourself what parts of you got lost or abandoned along the way. This could include but is not limited to the following:

- Trusting your gut
- Dreams
- Liking who you are
- Emotions
- Playfulness
- Body image
- Ability to have fun
- Peace
- Femininity
- Confidence

What parts do you miss the most? What parts do you want back? What is the part of you that you are afraid you will never get back? Don't give up. Keep searching for her. She didn't die. She's there. She just needs enough safety to come out.

Remember that you get to take up space in this world and that you have great worth and value. That is not tied to whether you are in a relationship, what your partner did or didn't do, or what he thinks of you. You have innate worth and value as a human being. No one can take that away or change it with their actions. It may not feel that way, but sometimes you have to fight those inner voices by speaking truth to the lies.

I recognize that for some, the idea of rediscovering who you are falls flat because you never had the opportunity to figure out who you were in the first place. That's okay. I often have clients in their sixties and seventies doing the brave work of discovering who they are. It's an honor to watch their eyes light up as they connect with themselves, find their voice, gain confidence in who they are, understand why they do what they do, and become comfortable in their own skin for the first time. As one woman stated about her journey of finding herself later in life: "Is it easy? No. But I'm glad I did it. I don't think it's too late to find happiness or to learn new things about yourself. I'm learning how to play at seventy-two-years old! I am coming into my own skin, and I am now more comfortable. It's freed me." It is never too late, and it is worth the effort to find yourself.

If you are unsure what you like to do, start experimenting. Search out random things you can do in your city. Find one that sounds interesting and try it. If you enjoy it, do it again. You can also reflect on your childhood and what you enjoyed doing then. Go back to those hobbies and see if you still enjoy them. Try things out and see what brings you joy.

As you discover yourself, find safe people who will encourage you in your pursuit. This is important because those who are used to you being a certain way may not be supportive of the changes at first, especially if these changes impact them. But remember, you have one life to live. You get to make your choices and live them out!

Redefining Safety

When betrayal happens, there is a shift in your felt sense of safety—with others and in the world. This most basic aspect of our existence takes such a profound hit. Many wonder if they will ever feel emotionally safe in a relationship again. It is normal to want your partner to provide safety, but after betrayal that can feel—or actually may be—impossible.

There comes a time, however, when safety must shift from the external to the internal. In other words, instead of others providing safety for you, you must learn to provide it for yourself first and foremost. This is a challenging statement, I know. We do, of course, need both external and internal safety. But when you develop an internal sense of grounding and empowerment, knowing you can trust yourself to take action when needed, it can provide a sense of calm that is deep and rooted.

Friendships

At a time when you need friends more than ever, most betrayed partners find themselves struggling in this area. The good news, though, is that what most women are looking for in friendships after betrayal is usually a healthier and more honest and transparent version of friendship.

After betrayal, most women are looking for a healthier and more honest and transparent version of friendship.

Here are a couple things to keep in mind as you work toward developing new friendships and strengthening your existing friendships.

Self-Talk

First, be aware of your self-talk. It will determine a lot of your actions. As Brené Brown reminds us, you don't have to be perfect to be worthy of love and belonging.[1] Tell yourself that, on repeat if needed, as you enter social situations. Most betrayed partners have experienced some degree of gaslighting and being told that they are crazy. This can result in you feeling defective and unworthy. Instead, tell yourself the truth: You are not defective, and you have great worth and value.

1. Brené Brown, *The Gifts of Imperfection: Let Go of Who You Think You're Supposed to Be and Embrace Who You Are* (Hazelden, 2010).

If you hear your partner's voice in your head putting you down, resist it. Name it for what it is—a remnant of your partner's unhealthy attempts to manipulate you. Then repeat to yourself that you do not have to be perfect to be worthy of love and belonging.

Changing patterns of self-talk and getting your partner's voice out of your head takes time. It is often a battle initially, so hang in there and keep speaking the truth to yourself when you are confronted with the lies (aka gaslighting and manipulation).

Risk

Second, you are going to have to take risks to form new friendships. Be the kind of friend that you want to have. This will undoubtedly require vulnerability and authenticity, both of which can be terrifying. Yet, even though these are scary to lean into, they *are* the gateway to freedom. All of this is unavoidable and requires great courage, but it is worth it.

When you take risks, however, you want to attempt them in the safest way possible. What that means for friendships is that you start by offering a little bit of yourself and see how others respond. If they respond with safety and kindness, you can be more vulnerable and, again, see how they respond. If they react poorly, you have your answer, and you can pull back. You can also watch how they talk about and treat others. If they do not treat others well, they are unsafe, and it will only be a matter of time before they treat you poorly.

Keep the bar high in friendships. No one is perfect, but you deserve kindness, safety, and authenticity.

You deserve kindness, safety, and authenticity.

195

Pockets of Pain

During the crisis of the earlier phases of betrayal healing, the pain is overwhelming. It is too intense and too much to process all at once, so it is normal to lock down certain aspects of the pain. This is an unconscious survival reaction that decreases the overwhelm to a more manageable level. In Phase Four, you may find some of these hidden pain pockets and even intentionally seek to bring them to the surface in order to find deeper healing.

To identify what you may have locked down, think back to things you've said and fill in the blank: *I'll never _____ again.* For example, *I'll never trust a man again. I'll never be naked around my partner again. I'll never go on vacation with him again. I'll never wear lingerie again.*

I call these pain pockets because they are pockets of wounds that are not healed. The problem is when you lock these things down, a part of your personality gets locked down with them. For instance, you can lose the trusting part of your personality when you lock down never trusting a man again. You can lose a sense of freedom when you lock down never being naked with your partner again. Now that you are in Phase Four and focusing on yourself, you may start to notice and miss these aspects of yourself.

Let me be clear that locking down pain is different from setting boundaries. You may choose not to be naked around your partner because he is not safe and would hurt you emotionally—or even physically—if you were. That is a healthy and wise decision. In that case, you are facing the pain and making a *conscious* choice about how to handle a situation. Pain pockets, on the other hand, are usually *unconscious* ways of protecting yourself, which ultimately block your healing from that situation. These areas remain locked down even though the danger has passed.

It is your choice whether to heal and reclaim your pain pockets. You can experience an incredible amount of healing without ever touching them. You may decide that digging out the pain to heal the last 15 percent is not worth it—or not worth it yet. You get to make that choice. No one gets to shame you or make you feel bad if you decide to leave well enough alone after all of the pain and hurt and the incredible effort you have already put into healing.

The reality is that healing pain pockets can feel scary. It is hard to go back and face the pain. Similar to what happens when we push aside our grief, the pain gets trapped at the level of intensity it was when you buried it, when you first locked it down, which means it will initially come back up with similar intensity. The good news is the intensity does not last long. When you bring it into the present, you can navigate it with all the healing you've learned, and it usually calms quickly. I want to honor the reality, however, that it takes courage to face it. If you get to a place where you want full healing and freedom—no matter how scary it is—then the pain pockets are the key.

It's important to know that you can heal your pain pockets whether or not you are still in the relationship. If the relationship is healing and he is safe enough, you may want to explain what you are doing and let him know how he can support you. Feel free to tell him what you need in the process, give him guidance as to how he can help, and share with him the things that would make the process of exploring pain pockets feel less scary. If you are no longer in the relationship or your partner is not safe, it may be helpful to have a counselor or trusted friend walk through it with you.

Healing a pain pocket could look something like this: You said that you would never trust a man again, so you start by simply opening yourself to the *idea* of trusting one—not in a romantic relationship but in another context. If you play a sport, perhaps you could find a safe male coach and learn to trust him. Then, perhaps you consider working with a male therapist and working out your fears and vulnerability in that context. You can start small and work your way up, allowing each new experience to expand upon the last. And, of course, if any man is not safe in that process, change directions and find someone else . . . but resist throwing the baby out with the bathwater and saying that no man can ever be trusted. There are good, safe men out there, but trust your gut in the process of finding them.

Making Peace with Your Body

Few betrayed partners make it through betrayal without it taking a heavy hit on their body image. The intimate betrayal feels incredibly personal, so it is hard not to compare yourself to the porn stars he was looking at or the affair partner he acted out with. Body image struggles can be relentless and painful.

Phase Four is when it's time to gently and compassionately face your insecurities and feelings about your body, if you haven't already. Your partner certainly did damage here, but your healing will now come from taking him, his actions, and his opinions out of the picture and focusing on how you view yourself, and then leaning into any areas of self-hatred or self-rejection you notice. This may be an area where counseling or EMDR could be helpful. Ultimately, though, the better you feel about yourself and your body, the less you will be triggered and the more peace and confidence you will feel. This can happen at any weight and any size. It is not about being perfect or any ideal physical state but about loving and accepting yourself.

It is also helpful to shift the focus from physical beauty to the idea of radiance. Beauty can be arbitrary, and its definition is constantly changing due to societal and cultural standards, age, and many other factors. Regardless, it is highly subjective, and it is not worth chasing. Instead, I want to offer the idea of radiance. I love this quote often attributed to actress Jane Seymour: "Beauty is a radiance that originates from within and comes from inner security and strong character." Redefining what beauty means to you can be a powerful step in healing.

Forgiving Yourself

Many betrayed partners feel they have betrayed themselves at some point throughout the process. When the dust settles, they may be left with a nagging disdain for themselves. In this phase, I offer the gentle suggestion to look at those areas in which you feel shame through the lens of compassion. Forgiving yourself can be the hardest and bravest thing you do. If you feel that hated flush of shame as you read this, I want you to know that you are not alone. Most women who have gone through betrayal have things they regret, so let's boldly face this together.

The most common way women feel they have betrayed themselves is by staying in the relationship after finding out about the betrayal. Often, women tell themselves—and even their partner—that if he ever cheated, she would be done immediately. This is said sincerely, but when it does happen, the realities and complexities of life have to be factored in, which can lead to a different outcome—whether for a season or for a lifetime.

Instead of beating yourself up, consider thanking your younger self for valuing you, keeping the bar high, and taking a stand for what you rightly deserve in a relationship—loyalty, faithfulness, kindness, safety, and love. Then have compassion on the part of you who had to face the life-altering devastation of betrayal. The one who had to fight for her reality. The one who was flooded with pain, anger, confusion, and sadness. The one who was trying to hold it together and make sense of life while caring for those who needed her. The one who had to face the financial fears and realities. I encourage you to offer that part of you the compassion and respect she deserves for making the best decision she could with what she had at that moment—whether that was the decision to stay or leave.

Betrayed partners may also feel the need to forgive themselves for things they did or said that they feel bad about. It may be you feel you prostituted yourself to your partner to try to save the relationship. Perhaps you watched porn with him when it went against your desires or values. Maybe you hit your partner or self-harmed after finding out about the betrayal. You might have yelled at your partner in front of the kids, and it scared them or gave them more information than they needed. Again, I offer compassion and encourage you to be gentle with yourself as you face this.

There are a few steps that will help as you move toward forgiving yourself. The first step is identification. Find a quiet space and open your heart and mind to the idea of forgiveness. Ask yourself if there is anything you need to forgive yourself for. Spend time in silence or journaling to see if anything comes to mind. This is not an area you need to spend much time digging into. If you have areas in which you need to forgive yourself, they will jump to the surface pretty quickly. Write them down. If nothing comes to mind, then move on.

The second step is to own it. Let's be honest: We all want to be perfect. We'd like to believe that our motives are always pure. But the fact is we are human. We fail ourselves and others. And when you add the pain and devastation of betrayal to the mix, things will get messy. Facing the things you are ashamed of head-on and accepting the reality that you are human and imperfect provide a foundation for forgiving yourself.

The third step is to speak it. Shame grows in secret, but it heals in the light when shared with safe people.[2] Think of one or two safe people in your life and tell them. It may be a counselor or a friend. If you don't have anyone right now, then look to build those relationships where it would be safe enough to let it out.

The fourth step is to take action where necessary. If you crossed a line with someone, apologize to them and do what you can to make

---

2. See Brené Brown, *Daring Greatly: How the Courage to Be Vulnerable Transforms the Way We Live, Love, Parent, and Lead* (Gotham Books, 2012).

it right. Safety comes first though. If it is not safe to be vulnerable with someone, then perhaps write a letter instead but don't give it to them. Remember that if you apologize to your partner, it does not mean you are apologizing for everything—or even anything— other than the specific area where you crossed the line.

The final step is to say out loud that you forgive yourself: "I choose to forgive myself for _____. I recognize that my actions had the following consequences: _____, and I commit to healing those areas when I can and where it is safe to do so." You may need to forgive yourself over and over again. That's okay. It is worth the effort to move toward forgiveness and compassion for yourself.

The goal here is freedom. Forgiving yourself is freeing yourself from shame, guilt, and self-hatred. It makes space for more joy and peace. Think back to your personal circle. The more ownership you take of your life, emotions, and decisions, the more freedom and personal power you will have. The more you nurture your relationship with yourself, the more peace you will feel.

Forgiving yourself is freeing yourself.

It's Time to Dream

It's time. It's time to live. It's time to dream. Remember, intimate betrayal shattered the good, but it also shattered the bad. You now have the freedom to take those broken pieces and create something new—a beautiful mosaic of your own design. Be intentional about the direction you want to go and the design you want to create, and then start putting the pieces in place one healing step at a time. Take your time, enjoy the process, and savor the beauty as it unfolds. This is the start of something new—not void of the past but built on the strength and resilience of everything you've learned along the way.

The Power of Healing

When I think of the power of healing and resiliency, one night will forever be etched in my mind: September 14, 2023. It was during the first retreat I led for betrayed partners. Nine strangers flew to Paris, France, for a six-day retreat focused on rebuilding and reengaging in life, beauty, and adventure. That evening we roamed through Trocadéro Square with a spectacular view of the Eiffel Tower twinkling in the background. The night was warm, and the air was filled with the life, energy, and music of a singer and his piano. The music drew us in, and a few bold ones from the group started dancing to the familiar American tunes he was playing. Soon the rest of the group joined in. The group's laughter and joy were infectious, and before long, a huge group of people from all over the world had joined us. Young and old were dancing together, and everyone was singing at the top of their lungs.

At one point, I stepped away from the singing and dancing and turned to face the Eiffel Tower to soak it all in. A deep sense of peace and contentment washed over me. I looked back at my group—those nine brave souls who had been strangers days before, now united by the shared experience of healing from intimate betrayal. All had felt lost, isolated, hopeless, and alone . . . and now they were laughing, hugging, and dancing together in the light of the Eiffel Tower. It was a magical night that demonstrated the power and beauty of healing and the deep resiliency of the human spirit.

Healing can—and does—happen. There is joy, laughter, beauty, peace, and adventure in life. And you do not need to go to Paris or dance in the light of the Eiffel Tower to make it happen. The most important healing is found inside of you. There is peace as you nurture your soul. There is power as you find your voice and set boundaries. There is freedom as you forgive and offer compassion to yourself and others. There is joy as you open your heart and connect with safe people. There is fun as you press back into play and adventure.

There is a good life ahead of you.

There is a good life ahead. This is your one life to live. Step into your power and go create a beautiful life that you are excited to live. I am cheering you on!

Tammy Gustafson

is a trauma-informed licensed professional counselor, coach, researcher, and speaker with over fifteen years of experience. She is passionate about helping women pick up the broken pieces of their hearts after intimate betrayal, find their strength, navigate the counterintuitive process of healing, and discover new ways to live with purpose, joy, and confidence.

Tammy holds a master's degree in counseling. She is the host of the Betrayal Healing Conference and leads retreats for betrayed partners to Paris, France. She is a certified EMDR therapist and is the founder and CEO of Betrayal Healing and LiveFree Counseling.

Tammy is a passionate indoor skydiver and Paris street roamer. She also enjoys adventuring in the Colorado mountains with her husband and kids.

Connect with Tammy:

🌐 BrokenToBraveBook.com

🌐 TammyGustafson.com

📷 @tammylgustafson

how to heal from it. She provides the encouragement and tools readers need to create a joyful, healthy future."

Jennifer Joy Freyd, PhD, Professor Emerit of Psychology, University of Oregon; Affiliate Professor of Psychology and of Gender, Women & Sexuality Studies, University of Washington; founder and president of the Center for Institutional Courage

"Approachable and supportive, *Broken to Brave* is a must-read for anyone who is experiencing the devastating impact of sexual betrayal. The author walks betrayed partners through the phases of healing, from the pain of D-Day all the way to thriving. What a treasure this book is! I'm really excited to recommend it to my clients."

Dan Drake, LMFT, CCPS-S, CCDG-M, CSAT-S, coauthor of *Building True Intimacy, Letters from a Sex Addict*, and the Full Disclosure series

"In *Broken to Brave*, Tammy Gustafson encourages and even challenges you to pick up the broken pieces of your life and courageously rearrange them into a beautiful new work of art. From the shattering pain of grief and loss, to the early stages of recognition and recovery, all the way through the transformational process of post-traumatic growth, Tammy draws deeply from her personal experience and clinical expertise to provide you with this faithful guide and rich resource. For anyone trying to heal from intimate partner betrayal, this empowering book is for you."

Clinton J. Nunnally, LPC